# 5 Minute eBay Descriptions That Sell

How To Make Money Selling Items On eBay
More Efficiently Using Highly-Effective
eBay Copywriting Tactics, Simple eBay
Selling Tips and Tricks, and Proven
Shortcuts That Save You Huge Amounts of
Time When Listing on eBay

Copyright © Robert Boduch
All rights reserved worldwide.

Cover image credit: © Paul Moore | Dreamstime.com

This product is sold with the understanding that the author and publisher take no responsibility in the business dealings pursued by readers and this manual makes no income guarantees whatsoever. As with any business or opportunity, success is largely a function of the reader's work ethic, actions, strategy, and ingenuity in implementing the information outlined herein.

It is recommended that the reader rely on his or her own judgment and experience in the utilization of any of the ideas, techniques, or suggestions contained in this volume.

Published by: Success Track Communications

thesuccesstrack@gmail.com

# TABLE OF CONTENTS

# Introduction

## My Aim For You In Writing This Book

Dozens and dozens, if not hundreds of books and courses specifically about "eBay" are already available on the market today. So I knew that simply writing another eBay book in general wasn't going to help a whole lot of people. This one had to be unique. It had to address the major challenges with making money on eBay... and it had to help others easily overcome the hurdles that limit their cash flow and profits.

If you've ever been on eBay as a buyer or seller, you already know how the system works. No need to help you through the registration process or to fill-in-the-blanks at each step along the way (eBay does a fine job of providing helpful support here).

If you've been a seller for some time, you've undoubtedly tasted and basked in some unexpected success. But I'm willing to bet that you've also had your fair share of frustrations too. Don't worry. I'm here to help you.

Even if you're an established seller, I hope to provide plenty of practical ideas and approaches to help you reach a new level of success.

There's little doubt that eBay can be a goldmine for any astute seller who pays attention to the market place, knows what others want, and can communicate effectively from a sales perspective. Think of the most successful sales professional you've even met. I can guarantee you that he or she demonstrated excellent communication skills. If you can capture and transfer some of these nuances to the eBay format, greater success is sure to follow.

Marketing in any medium is about communication and connection. It's about building relationships with people that are mutually beneficial. On eBay, building a relationship with buyers and using past experiences to make a positive impression on new customers is a critical component.

Apply your most valuable sales knowledge and skills to each listing as though you were face to face with a single customer. But unlike this one-on-one scenario, eBay exponentially expands your sales efforts to reach a global audience.

> *"Stripped of nonessentials, all business activity is a sales battle. And everyone in business must be a salesman."* -- Robert E. M. Cowie

Selling on eBay is salesmanship multiplied to the nth degree. In this fashion, it's similar to direct response marketing. But unlike typical direct response sent to a narrowly-defined mailing list, your potential exposure is unlimited in its reach. Your audience is global in nature and your sales message is out there 24 hours a day, for the duration of each listing.

Never before in history has the individual entrepreneur had so wide a reach, such unlimited marketing power and potential for profit working from a single computer, in the corner of a spare room.

Just think about that power for a moment.

eBay gives you unprecedented and unlimited opportunity. At any hour of any day, you can create a listing to sell just about anything. Once posted, your listing is accessible to anyone who's interested, wherever they happen to be.

eBay enables you to compose a simple listing, post it, and have it work tirelessly around the clock for as many as ten days at a time (or longer with an eBay Store). You have the capability to reach hundreds of potential buyers for mere pennies each time. And for every item you list, you potentially reach another audience that's just as eager to pursue it.

There's no limit to how far you can ride this thing. You can repeat the process with many different items, as often as you want. What makes eBay exceptional as a marketing venue is that you get to make your most compelling sales presentation every time. You don't have to worry about forgetting an important detail or key point, spewing out a canned pitch, or meeting your potential buyer face-to-face and sweating bullets when asked a difficult question. No, no, no! You can think through your listing and polish it up before unleashing it to the masses.

Simply provide your most important item information in an appealing way. Each time a prospective buyer checks out your listing, your best salesperson emerges confidently… energetically… and inexpensively.

Never before has such financial power been available to anyone with a computer and internet connection. eBay represents a revolutionary opportunity to build a global business from your basement. You can reach out to people around the world within minutes and sell to those you probably couldn't affordably contact any other way.

What's really terrific about selling on eBay is that you control your level of activity. You can ramp up your efforts… or scale back to any degree, according to your schedule and personal preferences. You can even pack it up and take it with you wherever you travel, should you so desire. Few, if any other moneymaking or business opportunities give you this kind of flexibility and portability.

## Where Most eBay Sellers Go Wrong

Some sellers make millions of dollars every year on eBay. Others are content to sell an item here and there and pocket a little spare change. Top sellers are pros who know what sells and have established connections with manufacturers and suppliers. They know how to create listings that get people to buy and their systems ensure healthy profits.

But this book is written for the remaining 98.7% of eBay sellers. I'm one of you. I've made some good money on eBay over the years. But I've also experienced the frustration of paying for listings only to find that my item didn't sell. "What's going on?" I wondered. "I thought anything would sell on eBay."

Truth is… pretty much anything under the sun – as long as eBay allows it – can and has been sold there. Items I wouldn't think of buying at any price (at least before I learned the secrets of huge profits on eBay) have sold for hundreds – even thousands of dollars. Yet frustration is fueled when an item you know in your heart is valuable and worth a considerable sum to you, remains unsold at the end of the auction.

That in itself is a valuable lesson. Just because you're attached to an item, or feel it's worth a lot of money to you, doesn't mean others will feel the same way.

What I've learned about making the most of one's own sales efforts on eBay is shared throughout this book. But a fundamental revelation to remember is this: most items don't generally sell themselves. Sure there are exceptions. And you can probably find examples yourself of items that fetched enormous amounts of money despite the rather lackluster advertising associated with it.

eBay being the marvel that it is can deliver huge profits without much in the way of a "killer" ad generating enormous amounts of interest and action. The reason for this is that some products are occasionally in such high demand from people who have already been "sold" that they'll even pay outrageous sums for certain merchandise.

But if you're banking on this, you're essentially setting yourself up for disaster. In fact, the myth that an item sells itself will lead to ruin more often than not for aspiring eBay profit seekers. A lucky score is great. But it's not a sound basis for creating a long-term income stream.

It's best to keep that underlying idea in mind as you create each individual listing. *Most items don't generally sell themselves.* Remember this and give it your best shot every time out and your bottom line results will improve.

To some, "sell" is a dirty word. They'll do almost anything to avoid it. Perhaps this is due to a deep-seated resentment of door-to-door salespeople, interruptive telemarketers, or used car sales types who will tell you just about anything you want to hear, in order to close the deal.

On eBay, you don't have to worry about face-to-face selling or the frequent rejection that goes with the territory. What you'll learn here will help you get better results by allowing your words and images to communicate effectively and convince others to bid or buy now. If you're up for that – this book is written for you.

Most sellers leave money on the table. They accept much less for their items than they could get, if they only applied effective sales psychology and basic, proven, copywriting principles to their listings.

The problem of items selling for much less than they should usually comes about as a seller rushes through the sometimes boring and tedious job of creating and posting an auction listing. They speed through just to get another item listed, in the hopes that its mere presence in the eBay marketplace will cause a stir and bring them another profitable sale.

That strategy might work if you're selling a product that's red hot in the marketplace and wanted by huge numbers of people. But it's a recipe for failure with most items.

Another dangerous approach is to throw together an ad just to get an extra item up on eBay. It's an easy trap to fall into – I've done so myself. You may very well sell your item. But even if you do, it will probably go for a lot less than it could have, had you taken even a few minutes to inject some selling power into your Title and Item Description.

Even conscientious sellers leave money behind with their listings because they simply don't have a good understanding of what it takes to create ad descriptions that make people want to bid and buy. They don't understand the basics of copywriting and so their ads lack persuasive power. Whatever the case may be, this resource will help make you more money from the same number of listings you would normally post on eBay each month. Keep reading.

## Every Listing Counts

Sellers want to generate sales and produce maximum profits. If you do that consistently, you'll have a successful eBay business that can grow to any level that suits you. You can operate part time to any degree… or make it your goal to meet and then surpass the income you would receive from a "regular" job.

In order to reach this level of sustained profit, it's necessary to take each individual listing as a serious component of your business.

Think of it this way…

If you operated a furniture store, you would surely recognize the importance of the room settings and layout of your showroom. If you had ten different, fully-furnished rooms, you wouldn't focus your attention on only one or two. Instead, you'd make each display room come alive with complementary fabrics, styles, and finishes, created at the hand of a skilled interior designer.

But one of the things I've noticed with eBay sellers is they tend to put forth a solid effort on occasion… and merely post plain-Jane listings the rest of the time. But I urge you to consider each and every listing as a potential moneymaker for you and to give it the time and attention it takes to do so.

There's a very good reason for doing so. You want to inspire people to go ahead and bid. With every ad, you want people to bid with confidence, rather than hold back in uncertainty. If you bail out before creating a decent listing, what kind of message does that send to your prospective customer?

Remember: your chief objective with every listing is to get people to eagerly bid with total confidence. Eliminate any second guessing by providing adequate details. Calm their fears by presenting yourself as a successful seller who has won over many customers in the recent past.

It's often a problem of time, or more specifically, a lack of time. For many, writing a strong item description can easily eat up an hour or two. And with no guarantees on a profitable return, it can be difficult to justify any significant time invested.

But creating effective eBay advertising doesn't require huge amounts of time. In fact, I'm going to show you how to write powerful, appealing item descriptions in just five minutes. It doesn't matter what the item is either. If you follow the ideas here, you'll be able to write five minute ads that attract more bids and higher selling prices – whenever you want.

## The Key To Successful eBay Advertising

Three key components make up a successful listing on eBay. These include...

> **1) Your Main Photograph** *(the one you'd select as your Gallery Image)...*
> **2) Your Title** and...
> **3) Your Item Description**

Each is an essential part of the whole. A weakness in any one component means you're left with a listing that cannot possibly deliver maximum profit to you. It's like trying to drive a car without brakes. You can get started down the road, but even a short trip will likely have disastrous consequences.

Focus on optimizing the power and effect of each of these "big three" components and you'll create listings with higher potential earnings. That's a major secret to success. It's my intention within these pages to help you integrate all 3 elements -- so your eBay ads produce superior results.

Even though a listing itself may cost just pennies, don't overlook the essentials of salesmanship each and every time. After all, you're hoping people will eagerly open their wallets and happily compete with others for a crack at your prized item.

The more often this happens, the more money you'll make. But each listing is viewed primarily by people who have never seen your ad before. So you have the opportunity to sell them, or send them away. Which result would you prefer?

Now, let's roll up our sleeves and dig in to the meat and potatoes of eBay Ad Magic, so you can start preparing powerful listings that make you a lot more money.

## Chapter One: Quick Start Guide To Writing 5-Minute eBay Ads That Sell

### Why A "Quick-Start" Guide?

The purpose of this chapter is to provide you with the basic information to bang out five-minute ads that make you money – starting today.

Success with the five-minute system means you'll be crafting solid, sensible and yet persuasive descriptions that move people to action. And it won't eat up much of your time.

In fact, with this Quick-Start, you could be up and running and using these techniques in minutes -- without having to go through every page of the text. Use this chapter plus the next two, to get started today. But be sure to come back and read the rest of the book later to get more detailed information and helpful tips.

Okay… now let's move forward.

There are a number of key points to creating powerful ads that sell – in just minutes. We'll examine each briefly and then dive right in to the specific details of the ad creation process.

When I first began developing this concept it seemed a little far-fetched. I was often frustrated by my inability to spit out ads quickly and efficiently for items of questionable potential returns. In other words, I didn't want to spend an afternoon writing details for an item that might only net me $50 to $100. That just wasn't an effective use of my time. But I had a houseful of stuff I wanted to sell, so I needed something better. I needed a faster means of getting a strong ad written and posted on eBay.

As I began mentioning this concept to others — particularly those with eBay sales experience, the first reaction was often one of disbelief. The whole idea of creating an eBay listing in five minutes is something almost every seller truly wants — but few believe (initially at least) is even possible.

My mission is to change that perception and to provide you with solid information that will help you get the job done in less time than ever before.

So let's get started with the things you need most.

# 5 Important Preliminary Steps

### 1. The right attitude.

Your attitude at the beginning of any task is crucial to your outcome. And it's no different when it comes to writing your eBay ad copy. If you assume the attitude that you can write a powerful ad in 5 minutes – your chances of success skyrocket.

But if you doubt yourself, you're only getting in the way of your own success. You need to have enough confidence in yourself and enough confidence in your item. It should no longer be a question of if you can pull this off because you absolutely can. But just in case you have any lingering doubts — your first result should be ample proof.

It doesn't matter how much experience you have writing ads of any sort or selling on eBay. Simply pay attention to the key principles that I'm going to share with you and give it your best shot. Be sure to have fun with this. I want you to be serious in your intention but lighthearted in your approach. I've found that if you just allow yourself to enjoy the process, the end result will be much more enjoyable to read for others -- and more effective and profitable for you. On the other hand, if it's a painful and arduous to write, you can imagine what it would be like for the reader.

### 2. Choose your goal.

Decide upfront the number of ads you're going to create in the next hour or that evening. Set your target and stick to it. Whatever number you decide upon should remain as your target for that session. This means that you need to be organized in your activities and avoid those time-wasting telephone calls and e-mails while you're busy creating your eBay ads.

It's okay to shoot for a lofty target. But in order to hit it, you need to work at maximum efficiency. Don't schedule your ad creation time when you've got too many other things on the go or you'll find it extremely difficult to focus. Clear off your desk so you have a clean slate with which to begin. Have your 10 or 15 items ready to go. This means cleaning your items, preparing them for your photo studio and having taken snapshots of all the items before you begin writing your ads.

### 3.  Focus on one item at a time.

It doesn't matter if you get 3, 10, or 103 items lined up ready to be listed on eBay. You can only tackle one ad at any particular time. So during your five-minute ad writing process, pay absolutely no attention to any other item but the one in front of you.

In our fast-paced world of unlimited choices, it can sometimes be a challenge to stay focused for any period of time. Have you ever set aside an hour to knock off a simple task, only to find at the end that you have little to show for your 60 minute investment?

Concentrating on a single element requires effort. Of course the more you do this the more effective you become at staying centered on a specific topic. Undoubtedly your first attempt at writing a five-minute ad will find your mind wandering here and there.

The real trick is to notice when you stray and to quickly make a course correction. You've only got five minutes to bang out an ad- that's the challenge. But to make the most of your efforts you need to stay focused on the task. What you want to do is condition your mind to get to the really good stuff quickly knowing full well that when the timer sounds, you're moving on.

### 4.  Uncover important details.

For you to write an ad of any sort, you need to know as much as possible about the product you're trying to push. If you wing it, you'll miss the mark.

Don't guess about product details, uncover them. Find the facts. This is the most important raw material available to you. That's why I always suggest having the item in front of you before you begin.

When a friend wants you to sell an item on eBay, insist on taking possession of that item before you spend any significant time on the job. You simply cannot understand a product at the same level by gathering your information from a distance. You need to have the item in front of you.

**Ask yourself a series of simple questions.**

> *What is it?*
>
> *What does it do or what is it used for?*
>
> *Is there a brand name?*
>
> *What is the condition of the item?*
>
> *How old is it?*
>
> *What is its color, size, model number?*
>
> *Is it for men, women, or children?*
>
> *What's different or unusual about this item?*

Quickly gather every potentially relevant detail you can. Take no more than a minute or two to capture the key information. This requires steadfast concentration, but if you do this effectively you'll be surprised by the amount of information you can gather in just one minute. Be sure to capture your findings on an audio recorder, or make written point-form notes.

No copywriter worth his salt would take a project on and start writing copy without first examining the product – and neither should you. It wouldn't matter if the task were to write an infomercial, sales letter, brochure, or eBay ad. You've got to begin with "what is" — the hard data pulled from the product itself before you can create a "what could be" scenario for the buyer.

Scope it out and gather as many pertinent details as possible. If you're not sure whether it's relevant or not, jot it down anyway. At this information-gathering stage your only concern is capturing any and every detail. After you've got it all recorded, you can then sort it out.

### 5.  Prioritize your information.

There's little doubt that some of the information you have is more valuable to a potential buyer than the rest. In order to capture the largest possible audience you need to deliver the most important points to the greatest number of people. If you were selling a lawn mover, for example — the condition, name brand, and size are probably much more important to the majority then the color. For some, color might be an important factor. But more people would consider the condition, brand, and overall size as being more significant to their decision to buy or bid.

The thing to remember here is to take the raw data you've collected and organize it in a simple sequence from the most important detail to the least. The reason for this is to capture maximum interest by focusing on the factors that are of greatest importance.

Prospects will only read as long as their interest is sustained. So it's crucial that you deliver the key information first before considering anything that may be of secondary significance.

## A Valuable Tool For Writing 5-Minute Ads

There's one piece of equipment I'm going to strongly suggest you pick up and use every time you sit down to craft an eBay ad. It's a pocket timer. It'll probably annoy you at first. But as you become accustomed to using it, you'll quickly appreciate its value. There's just no other way to limit your ad creation time accurately to just five minutes, without the use a timing device.

The timer I prefer is an interesting little device called the Invisible Clock by Time Now Corporation. You can find them on Google. It's probably the Cadillac of pocket timers and it's a beauty.

All you need is a simple device that counts down from five-minutes and then sounds a tone of some kind as time expires. A dollar-store model will get you started and in fact, may be enough for you. But a timer is an important tool for using these techniques. And if you plan to write lots of ads, you might want to consider an upgrade to the Invisible Clock.

Okay, so you're ready to begin your ad creation session. You've got a positive, expectant attitude, a method to record ideas and information, and a pocket timer.

## One More Thing

You're almost ready. There's just one more thing.

You've got to feel energized if you want to create your best work. Do not attempt to write any kind of advertising if you're feeling tired or lethargic. You'll tend to shortcut the process, have difficulty concentrating and in the end you won't be happy with the result. It's important to approach the task with a high energy level, a positive, expectant attitude and clarity of thought.

A great way to break out of the doldrums is to go for a run or brisk walk. Or if you're so inclined, have a workout. Another way to bring more oxygen to your brain and to give you a feeling of well-being and vitality is to do some simple deep breathing exercises. The easiest of these is to simply take a deep breath, hold it for a count of three... exhale and again hold your breath for a count of three. So you breathe in and hold it, then breathe out and hold it. Now repeat this process three to five times in a row and you'll notice that your energy level has risen.

Now with a clear head and energized spirit you're ready to begin.

## It's About Getting Bids, Making Sales, and Earning Long-Term Profits

My intention here is to help you create sensible, straightforward, and compelling advertising that sells products.

Selling is the name of the game. But it's important that it be done ethically. Your mission with each and every ad you prepare is to close the sale.

But your overall purpose is to gain a customer. You want customers to return time and time again to buy from you and the only way you'll do that is when your customers are entirely happy with their respective purchases. That's a proven way to achieve long-term success on eBay.

## Copy and Images Should Work Together

As a copywriter, I tend to be more word-oriented. Conversely, I suspect that most photographers and graphics specialists would tend to be image-oriented. But the reality of eBay is that both words and images are important and the most effective use of each is a combined approach where words and images work together to make the sale. The best eBay listings use both elements effectively to achieve this desired result.

Some people believe they need to be "creative" in order to generate effective eBay listings. But the fact is... you don't have to knock your market's socks off with creativity in order to make more sales at higher prices. In fact, an overly creative approach can actually be a detriment. Just concentrate on creating simple, effective, honest ads that get the job done. That's what it's all about. Not creativity for the sake of being creative.

## The 3 Keys To Guaranteed Sales Success on eBay

There are three simple secrets that will virtually guarantee your success in selling products on eBay:

> 1. Sell items that large numbers of people actually *want*.
>
> 2. Decide what it is about your specific item that makes it *important*, *unique*, and *of value* to the buyer.
>
> 3. Effectively *communicate* what it is that makes your item unique, important, and of value to the buyer.

If you keep these three simple steps in mind, you'll create the kind of results you want. You'll attract larger audiences of interested, eager prospects who would love to snap up whatever it is you have to offer.

By learning how to craft simple, powerful ads, you'll draw more attention to your listings. And that in turn tends to drive bids skyward, netting you a larger piece of the profit pie. Not a bad trade-off for discovering and applying the secrets of advertising that sells.

Success on eBay means selling your item at a price that represents a tidy profit. Like any business, it's all about making the sale at a point that's profitable.

The five-minute strategy gives you a solid basis from which you can build a successful eBay business of any size. Should the five-minute strategy be used every time? No. Sometimes you'll want to go all out and craft a lengthy sales letter to extract maximum earnings over the long haul. But with a solid understanding of the fundamentals, you can easily expand into more detailed ad copy.

The purpose of the five-minute process is to make creating your eBay listings quick, easy, and more profitable — regardless of your past frustrations and struggles.

## Is The "Five-Minute" Solution A Good Fit Here?

You need to make a decision at the outset. Does a five-minute ad work here, in this particular situation? In other words, is this an item that you can profitably sell by using only a five-minute ad?

Be reasonable in your assessment. If you want to take more time and provide a much more detailed description, that's quite all right. There will still be many more opportunities where the five-minute approach will be a perfect fit, so you can post more ads in less time.

Even if you want to go all out with a larger ad, it's a good idea to begin with five-minute copy. It will provide a solid footing from which to grow.

Have fun with this process. Create your listings in a spirit of adventure. Try unique approaches and test them out. You'll discover how effective your ads are in a matter of days.

If results are good, all you have to do is more of the same. If not, it could mean that enough people didn't see your ad the first time around, or it could mean your approach didn't work well. No big deal. Use the experience gained from each listing to guide your future decisions.

Learn from every result and adapt your approach. That's how you gain considerable skill at this task in very little time.


## Anyone Can Do This

Preparing eBay ads that sell isn't an art – it's a skill. Contrary to popular belief, it doesn't take a huge amount of creativity, as it does for someone who paints, sculpts or writes novels. Writing eBay ad copy is a vocational skill like cooking, carpentry, or auto mechanics. Therefore, it's something anyone can learn.

Throughout the eBay Ad Magic package I've shared ideas to help you specifically with your eBay ads. There's enough information and assistance here to help you get great results, even if you've never written anything more than a single-line classified ad before.


## Communicate Simply and Directly

Start with the basics and keep things simple. That's the underlying premise to the five-minute approach. You simple don't have time to meander. Instead, you're challenged to deliver only the most important information in a compelling way.

There's simply no time for award-winning creativity. In fact, such a route on eBay would probably have a reverse effect anyway.

Unless you're a gifted artist, striving to be "creative" can put an unpleasant and unnecessary pressure on you. Personally, drawing anything more than a simple stick-man is an exercise in futility for me. If I had to rely on my artistic skills I'd be living on the street.

Thankfully, I've found a system that works like a charm on eBay and that's exactly what I'm sharing in this course.

Begin with the proven basics. If you want to get fancy later on, that's entirely up to you. At any rate, I urge you to get started with the tried and true methods that have already been proven effective. With the right stimulus, anyone can be creative enough to compose a powerhouse ad on eBay.

## Simple Steps To Writing Five Minute Ads That Sell

Okay, let's begin crafting a five-minute ad. The first step is to get prepared.

Now is the time to get warmed up, so here's a simple 3-minute mental exercise. Get out a pen and blank piece of paper and get ready to write down as many uses for the product I'm about to reveal. Set your timer for 3 minutes and be prepared to stretch your mind.

What I want you to do is take 3 minutes to come up with as many uses as possible for....

*Vinegar*

Ready... set... go!

Think about it. Let your mind run free. Focus on this one product and imagine it as one of the most versatile everyday products ever developed. Strive for five different uses – more if you're on a roll.

At the three-minute mark – stop.

Did you come up with at least five different uses for vinegar?

Congratulations!

If not, don't worry about it. Shake it off. Maybe "vinegar" wasn't a good example for you. If that's the case, try something else like a penny… or a clothes hanger… or an apple... or maybe even those fabric-softening sheets you use in the dryer.

But whatever item you choose for this simple warm-up exercise -- don't sweat it. The idea is to open your mind... not shut it down.

Let your imagination take over. See how useful a simple item can become. That's the key to finding solid value in any item you plan to sell on eBay.

Find value where it isn't obvious to buyers. Bring it to the forefront so they can grasp these benefits themselves and your item will have much greater appeal in the marketplace. More people will want it and that will in turn drive up the selling price.

A hidden advantage of this simple warm-up exercise is that it proves that you've got what it takes to find the buried treasure in any product. It's almost always there. You just have to look for it. And you've just proven yourself capable.

A preliminary step to the writing of any ad is product research. For our purposes on eBay, we'll keep it short and simple.

It's now time to gather information about your item. No it's not the most fun and exciting part of writing copy... but it is the most important. You need to know all you can about whatever it is that you're selling. So resist any temptation to skip over this fundamental step.


## Research Made Easy

Here's a way to make basic research bearable for anyone. Limit your time spent researching to a quick minute or two. Once again, a timer comes in handy for this. Place the item in front of you and set your timer for one minute.

In that one minute period, record every detail about the product that comes to mind. Remember, your listing is only effective when it sells at a profit. But in order to sell any item, you have to provide information. Reveal the key details that will help prospective buyers decide in favor of placing a bid now.

Go deep. Look for more information than most sellers would ever find. Dig for details and jot everything down. Don't stop because you think you've got enough information already. Keep going until the timer sounds. Having lots of raw data makes writing a great ad that much easier and faster.

Look at everything as a source of helpful information. In addition to the product itself, consider any or all of these elements that may also be present:

- Product packaging
- Instructions
- Manufacturer's website
- Catalogues
- Competitors' ads (on eBay and elsewhere)
- Product specification sheets
- Certificates of authentication
- Original bill of sale

## Quick Questions To Point You In The Right Direction

As you ponder an item you're about to put up for sale, here are some key questions to help you extract important information you'll want to use in your eBay listing. Refer to these whenever you get stuck.

1. What is it?

2. How is it used, or how does it work?

3. Where is this used?

4. Is there a brand name?

5. What size is it?

6. Is there a specific model number or name?

7. What year was it made or published?

8. What is the most important issue when buying this kind of product?

9. How is this item better than others?

10. Describe any obvious physical characteristics.

11. What do you think is this item's greatest attribute?

12. What do sellers overlook when promoting a product like this?

13. What problem does it solve?

14. How reliable is it? How long will it last as compared to others?

15. Is it economical? How so?

16. What is the approximate value?

17. What will be your starting bid?

18. Who used this before and what do they have to say about it?

19. Will you guarantee the item?

20. Who is most likely to buy? Why?

21. What is their main concern when buying this type of product? (Example: price, reliability, quality, efficiency, authenticity, availability, etc.)

22. Will your ad appeal to multiple groups of prospects?

23. How will this item make your buyer feel great?

## Don't Forget Important Details

In ad writing in general – and especially on eBay – specifics sell. So capturing as much raw data as you possibly can in such a short time period provides you with plenty of ammunition to use in your ad copy.

Once collected, it's time to sift through the information and prioritize it. Shuffle through your collection of data. It's important to think from your prospective buyer's viewpoint. What are the most important details your target buyer needs to know? What will give them the feelings they crave?

Think about how your item will make them feel *smarter, successful, attractive, confident, in control, youthful, wealthy,* or *relieved.* Then, make this the focal point of your ad copy.

Choose your top 5-7 points and number them, beginning with the most important (as far as buyers are concerned) and working your way on down through the list.

Your list of key points could vary considerably from one item to the next. For example, if you were selling a set of gently-used car tires, your key information might include...

- Size
- Brand
- Condition
- Quantity
- Location (Due to high shipping costs)

What buyers are likely interested in is peace of mind driving with quality tires at a fantastic price. An ad that reflected this would likely do quite well.

If you were selling a first edition book, none of the above would come into play, with the exception of the *condition* of the item.

Recently I listed a "first edition" copy of James Michener's *Tales of the South Pacific*. What was important to bidders was this:

- Authentication (Copyright, Printing, Publisher Details, Size)
- Overall Condition
- Condition of Dust Jacket

Buyers wanted verification that the book was an authentic first edition more than anything else. Clearly they were collectors looking to add a rare piece at a bargain price.

So the trick to crafting a five-minute ad that does the job for you is to understand both the market and enough about your item to deliver the key details right up front — without requiring interested prospects to have to ask you for it.

## Turn Facts Into Irresistible Advantages

Take your most important facts pertaining to your item and transform these into advantages of significance to the buyer.

The idea here is to turn mundane facts into statements that grab attention and stimulate an emotional response.

Instead of describing your silk tie as "red" – embellish that fact with a more vivid description such as *"luxurious, super-smooth, ruby red"*. See the difference? One sounds a little more inviting than the other. If you do this with every point, chances are you'll interest more prospects.

There are numerous ways to transform your raw data into interesting ad copy in just minutes.

A sure bet is to string together your most important benefits into a couple of paragraphs that paint an attractive, even irresistible image of your item and what the buyer can look forward to, should they win it.

Telling the story behind your unusual item can also create huge interest and a surge of traffic to your auction listing.

## Identify Your Best "Hook"

Think about the end result of owning your amazing item and emphasize the payoff that only one lucky winner will get to enjoy.

As human beings, we're emotional creatures and are therefore wired to move in a direction that feels good. It's that ego gratification that should be addressed first, before the logical facts come into play. Get the interest level up from the get-go and your prospect will be much more attentive and receptive to your message.

What's the one thing you could say about your item to attract attention and trigger genuine prospects to want to know more? That's the hook… and it should play a prominent role in your ad.

That's what you need to mention in your title, if possible. It's a challenge with such limited space, but it's also the key to receiving the maximum number of page views, multiple bids, and higher profits.

Set your item apart from every other. Identify what makes it unique and more valuable than any other and bring that information out, front and center.

It's this *value* that makes others take notice. Value is of prime importance and therefore, this specific information needs to assume a starring role in every production — in order to communicate this key detail quickly and effectively.

Give your audience solid reasons to bid or buy now. What makes your item worth more money… or how does it offer a unique advantage?

That's what you need to emphasize clearly and dramatically. Be sure to back up your benefits by stating the corresponding features. Features are supporting details that add validity to the emotional benefits of ownership. Your item's features act as proof so your overall message is more readily accepted as truth.

Stimulate action. Encourage browsers to bid now. Close the deal by reminding prospects of the unique and valuable advantages and the limited availability because your auction won't last long.

There's just nowhere else they can go to get the exact same item and within days, someone's going to own it – so it might as well be them. Of course, they'll need to act fast, or risk losing out on the gem you're offering.

If it's a typical eBay auction without a reserve price, you really should point this fact out. The easiest and most direct way to accomplish this is with a simple statement like this – *"With no reserve price in place, any bid can win... so bid now!"* As your description winds down, you've got one last chance to influence others to take action so you may as well take full advantage of the opportunity.

Think of your ad as having three parts – the image, title and description. All 3 should work together to present an accurate and captivating offer to interested prospects.

## Provide A Clear Visual Image Of Exactly What The Buyer Gets

Present a visual of your item as clearly and cleanly as possible. This is very important. Let interested prospective buyers see exactly what they'll get should they win. Make it as appealing and pleasing to the eye as possible because a clear, revealing photograph speaks volumes.

Use multiple shots when warranted. Your first choice should be your Gallery Image.

## Compose A Title That Gets Noticed By The Right People

Feature two or more of your item's most appealing keywords in the title, then add a dose of emotion by succinctly delivering a key benefit. Present the most relevant and important information you can fit into the title field.

Your Title and Gallery Image working together must accomplish these 3 critical tasks:

   **1. Capture attention**

   **2. Target your prospective buyers**

   **3. Deliver enough information to get true prospects to click-through to your full item description**

Think of your image and title as one entity – like a display ad or billboard. You want them to work together. Deliver a great shot of your item... but remember it's only a "thumbnail" edition photograph — until it gets clicked on.

So… when you get right down to it, you've got one image and a small handful of words to employ to draw prospective buyers inside.

Like a highway billboard, traffic goes whizzing by at a high rate of speed. And you've got just one shot at stopping prospects in their tracks and luring them inside where they can get the complete details on whatever you're offering.

To achieve all three tasks, a winning title includes important keywords, while at the same time communicating the item's most appealing advantage. It's best if you can include important keywords and make a bold benefit statement. But it's never an easy thing to do since the Title field is limited to just 55 characters. Nevertheless, I encourage you to strive for this ideal every time.

Be sure to insert keywords first however, since that's the main way people search for wanted items these days. If you limit your title to a benefit message without the keywords, you're shooting yourself in the foot by limiting the amount of quality traffic you might have otherwise attracted.

If you're struggling at the title stage, ask yourself...

1. **Who is the ideal target buyer for this item?**
2. **What would turn an interested prospect into an active bidder?**
3. **What makes this item rare, unusual, or worth more money?**

Arrange and then rearrange your words until you've filled the 55-character space with the strongest, most appealing line of words you can muster. Compose a title that makes prospects want to know more. It's got to be clear enough, yet intriguing or inviting at the same time.

## Hold Nothing Back In Your Item Description

Next... bring all the benefits to life, starting with the specific benefit that yields the greatest pulling power. What one advantage or attribute gives you the greatest marketing clout? This is where you must start.

Capture the interest and imagination of people with vivid, even dramatic descriptions of the special benefits and advantages your item offers. Add color and flair. Engage target buyers.

When you get down to the writing, it's quickly apparent why you need to get to know each item extensively as a preliminary step. After some experience, this gets easier as you understand the kinds of things to look for that are sure to capture the attention and interest of prospective buyers.

Your *Item Description* is where you have free reign and unlimited space to produce sales copy that interests, inspires, and compels people to take positive action. Include every pertinent detail. Present as complete a selling message as you can compose in the five minutes you've allowed – or whatever time you feel justified in investing in your ad copy.

Details are important. Weave your words into an interesting message buyers want to read. Add proof to enhance believability. Deliver plenty of benefits to induce interest with an emotional impact. And then bring it all to a natural close.

That first minute or two spent in research is the key because it gives you the foundational knowledge that's essential to accurately capture the value and uniqueness of any product. It also gives you the confidence to move into the ad creation process without reservation. When you've uncovered the key points of any product, you can step right up and write ad copy with authority because you know exactly what you're talking about.

Your fact-finding research is enough to clearly describe any item — in most cases. Then it's simply a matter of presenting a handful of attractive benefits to the buyer.

What having, using, or owning your item means to people on an emotional level is almost always more important than what it means logically. Think about that. And don't ever forget it.

Features are facts – specific, physical characteristics about your item. Benefits are what the buyer gets as a result of owning it. And most of the time we don't simply buy things — we buy what we imagine those things will do for us. It's that new and improved feeling we think we'll get that drives our buying activities. Understanding and applying this information will make you a far more successful eBay seller.

Give special prominence to those benefits that are unique to your item. Describe them in your own colorful way. Perception is everything. So it's important to bring out as much extra value in your items as you can extract. Stress benefits no one else is using. Of course, the more you know about the product and how others are marketing it, the easier this is to accomplish.

**Add Credibility To Your Claims**

Use product reviews, testimonials, or actual "hands-on" experience to back up your benefit claims. If your item has related documentation like a certificate of authenticity — be sure to show it visually, in addition to a snapshot of the item itself. Any credible proof you can present adds to the validity and acceptability of your sales points.

You can increase your chances of getting more bids by offering extra incentives. Strong incentives such as bonus reports, web references, or plain English instructions can help to enhance the perceived value of an item.

Consider offering a guarantee or a product return policy. Offer multiple payment options too. The idea here is to methodically eliminate the reasons why your prospect would not buy. When there's no sane reason not to move forward and there's no obvious obstacle in the way — your chances of getting multiple bids and higher closing prices increases substantially.

Descriptions can consist of a series or sentences or paragraphs. Or it could include a numbered or bullet-point list. Subheads are another visual tool you could employ to keep people reading your message, once you get them to your page.

It's the title that targets prospects with telegraphic keywords. Once prospects click-through, your powerful headline adds emotional interest. Used this way, the title and headline work together to attract the right prospects and increase their desire.

## How To Write Powerful Item Descriptions Quickly

Begin your description by expanding on the title with a more emotionally-engaging headline. Then... simply elaborate on your headline. Add to the impact with specific details of your featured item. Inject a testimonial or two to add credibility and power to your sales presentation.

How you write your description is really up to you. The choices are many.

You could...

- State 3-5 main benefits and follow it up with a list of the key features

- Expand on each segment of the main headline in detail by using the same voice, but enthusiastically building on each part

- Tell your own story

- Tell the story of someone else who used the product

- Create a numbered list of "reasons why" a prospect should bid or buy-it-now

- Present your item as the best solution or remedy

- Show a "Before" and "After" image… and tell how it works in your ad copy

## Valuable Sales Copy In Minutes

Your description could be a few paragraphs long, or multiple pages. If you stick to the 5-minute format, your ad should run anywhere from ½ page to a full page in length. Regardless of length, be sure to communicate with confidence and make it as compelling as possible. Exude genuine enthusiasm and you'll find your written descriptions are much more alive.

Strive to make your ad flow smoothly for easy, uninterrupted reading. Pack as much promise and meaning as possible in just 5 minutes of writing. Stay upbeat, enthusiastic and positive about the exceptional item one person is about to land.

If your item solves a problem, mention the problem, but don't dwell on it. Instead, focus 90% of your communication on the solution and how the buyer will feel by simply coming out on top when all is said and done.

Your mission is to get everyone who reads your listing to actually take positive action and place their bid. So pull out all the stops.

## Make It Even Stronger

Add extra incentives where possible. Stress the limited availability of your item. Your 7-day auction is a small window of opportunity for all interested parties. If they don't act now and reach for your rare item, they could miss out on something they'd truly love to own. Eliminate the hurdles so anyone can bid.

Be willing to ship internationally. Most overseas buyers understand they'll have to pay more for shipping and many will gladly do so. You should accept Paypal, as well as any other method of payment you're comfortable with and capable of providing.

Provide all the information the majority of buyers need to make an informed decision. Pump up your own enthusiasm before you sit down to write for five minutes. Pack tons of valuable information into a few paragraphs and your ads will be read.

## Review and Refine

After you've written your ad, edit for rhythm and flow. Correct any unplanned stoppages. Divide your written ad into bite-size sections that can be handled in one take by any reader. Vary the length of your sentences. After three to five lines of text, begin a new paragraph. This may take a few minutes more… or your copy may be good to go already.

Make it easy on the eyes with plenty of white space, sub-heads (where appropriate) and other visual devices such as bullet points and text boxes.

Write like you speak. That means beginning sentences with "and" and "but" or even using the occasional one-line paragraph. This provides a refreshing change of pace that keeps readers reading.

## Give It Your Best Shot

Writing 5-minute ads can be the breakthrough you've been looking for on eBay. Now there's no longer any excuse not to get those items you've been accumulating up on the auction block.

Now you too can craft ads efficiently and profitably. This gives you a tremendous advantage in this lucrative marketplace. With this system, at least you won't be investing tons of time writing ads for items that may not pay a sufficient dividend.

Look for items that can earn you good money with a five minute ad. By the way, these items are everywhere. All you have to do is look around to spot fresh new opportunities.

## Chapter Two: Small, Easy-To-Write Ads That Work Like Magic

Qualities of Short and Effective eBay Listings
Get Started Early
Provide Enough Information
Setting Yourself Up For Success
Think "Classifieds" First – Here's Why
The Half-Page Ad

eBay listings aren't just comprised of photographs. It's true that clear images communicate value information about your item, but images alone can't deliver the results of a listing that encompasses all three elements in an effective way.

Recently, the Millard Group surveyed 50,000 online buyers and more than half of them complained that the products were not clearly shown online when they made their purchases. But it wasn't the photographs that were to blame in most instances.

Words are a necessary accompaniment to paint a clearer image and clarify what the buyer is actually going to get. And in so many cases, the words used by sellers do an inadequate job of describing the details.

Add the detail that's not apparent from photos alone.

Demystify the product by explaining important details in simple terms. Is it a CD or printed book you're offering? A stock photo of the cover doesn't tell the buyer which it is. Only words can do that. Use images and words correctly and you'll make more money every time.

## Qualities of Short and Effective eBay Listings

### 1) Capture Attention.

Effective advertising captures the attention of qualified buyers. Every ad in any medium has to first capture the attention of interested and qualified prospects. To get attention means interrupting your prospects searches in order to direct them to your specific item listing.

eBay represents the world's largest inventory of products and that inventory changes on a daily basis. Buyers just don't know what sellers will be serving up next and so they tend to check in on a regular basis so they don't miss out on that one special item they'd just love to have.

So off those eager buyers go to eBay to see what might be available. Most will use the Search function while others will wade through a bunch of listing titles in their favorite category. Regardless of the search method used, buyers are served up a long list of titles. Some are accompanied by Gallery Images, while others are not.

But that's all any seller has to capture the attention of interested prospects. It's just one line of text -- just 55 characters -- and perhaps a single thumbnail image. That's it. And this either pulls prospects in or sends them along to continue their treasure hunt. In one brief line you need to attract qualified, interested and action-oriented people – and as many of them as you can each time out.

### 2) Build Interest.

Once you've stopped potential buyers in their tracks and temporarily interrupted the 'noise' competing for their attention, you've got to make their attention stick. Interest them or you lose them. Nobody's got a spare moment anymore. Grab them instantly or they're gone for good.

You've aroused curiosity and piqued interest with a strong title. Now it's time to strengthen that interest and squash any doubts. The first thing potential buyers want when they click through is verification. Is the item really what they hoped? You can begin to address this by expanding on your title straight away.

### 3) Describe major benefits and key features.

It's not just what your item is – but what it does that counts.

Benefits address the true value of an item from the buyer's perspective. It's the emotional payoff that far exceeds the actual cost. Paint a picture of what could be theirs.

But don't just cover the benefits. Many items are sold on eBay because the specific features offered are exactly what the buyer was searching for.

Features are easy to include. All you have to do is examine the product and list such details as brand name, model number, size, where it was made, color, year of manufacture, materials used, condition, and anything else you can think of that might be relevant to a single prospect.

Most sellers do an acceptable job of listing an item's features, but they fail to add any sales sizzle by graphically communicating the glorious benefits that make an item appear to be worth much more than the cost.

Every feature has at least one corresponding benefit you can extract and highlight in your item description.

Fail to do so and you can only hope for the prospects full recognition and appreciation of this value.

## 4) Create the desire to buy.

The trick to successful advertising is to create an overwhelming desire for ownership. On eBay, this means fanning the flames of desire until they're moved to bid or Buy-It-Now.

Make prospects feel the advantages. Allow them to mentally experience all those positive feelings and to unconsciously take ownership of the goods. Once they've crossed the threshold, it's no longer a question of whether it's something they truly want. And the more you can intensify the desire, the more money they'll be willing to spend.

## 5) Offer a way out.

In all buying environments and situations, most people have a deeply-rooted fear of being ripped off. With scams of all kinds being exposed regularly in the media, it's an issue that's forever at the forefront of collective consciousness. To ignore this is to self-inflict unnecessary harm to your business.

No honest seller would rip off anybody. But everyone senses that potential danger lies around any corner and thus people are wary of dealing with you for the first time. Build as positive a feedback rating as you possibly can to present a credible image of one who's worthy of their business. If a buyer feels they got the short end of the stick, the seller should expect to receive negative feedback. No serious business-oriented seller wants a negative blemish on their record and therefore is unlikely to purposely take advantage of a customer.

But most potential buyers want additional reassurances. They want to know that if they ever have a problem, they could return the item and get a refund. Guarantees are like a safety valve. They relieve the inner pressure and conflict potential buyers encounter at the moment of truth. Give people a way out with some kind of a guarantee, and they'll be more likely to step up and place a bid.

### 6) Make it a bargain.

A big part of the magic of eBay is the bargains it delivers every hour of every day. It's the first place millions go when they're looking for a great deal on a particular item.

Start your auctions at "regular" prices and you'll attract a much smaller audience than you would if the opening bid was a mere fraction of its true retail value. It takes a leap of faith to do this without having a Reserve Price in place. But if you're offering items that there's a noticeable market for and you follow these simple guidelines, you needn't worry about selling at prices that are too low.

You could in fact, end up with a much higher selling price. If you've got multiple units of the same product… or you own the rights to a published information product, you can continue to list them in the same way. Your closing price will vary between auctions. Some will end higher than you might have imagined while other listings won't attract the same level of interest and will close at a lower selling price. But what's important is the range of prices.

Look at the average selling price. If it's acceptable to you, keep doing more of the same. If not, look for ways to improve your listing and attract a larger audience. But don't forget to offer a bargain from the start.

Bargain prices make it easy to bid, rather than wait. If they don't bid right away, the chances of your prospects bidding at all plummets. Sure, some will mark the page as one to watch, with the intention of returning later and possibly bidding at that time. But as you know, they are no shortages of auctions to bid on at any given moment. It's easy to get distracted or to find another item that tickles their fancy. Most only have a limited amount of cash to spend. If you don't get their commitment early, it may be too late.

Remind them of the action they need to take if they want your item. Stir them into action so they have a shot at winning the item. One thing I often do is remind my prospective buyers that the odds are in their favor. I start the bidding as low as possible. Then I conclude with this simple statement "With NO RESERVE any bid can win." It's a simple nudge – a call to action. What it does is make prospects think twice before moving on.

Since the item is so inexpensive, they have nothing to lose by bidding now. And without a reserve price, even a single bid at the opening price could take home the goods. If the desire for the item is strong enough, this copy device is effective.

Finally, I like to conclude with a reminder of all the other related auctions I have on the go that this particular prospect might be interested in. Here's where specializing in one or two related categories works well. If I had 27 other items up, but they were all very different in nature, this technique wouldn't work too well at all.

But if I was selling a set of golf clubs and 25 of the other 27 items I had on eBay were golf accessories, they're a perfect match. All I would do is mention that I have a bunch of other golf items at the end of the item description and provide a link to the page that lists all my other auctions.

Now that is a powerful technique for maximizing the value of each individual listing. Give them more of the kind of stuff they're already interested in and bingo – you'll automatically draw more attention to all your items. Interestingly, you'll get more multiple item purchases, which reduces your labor at the shipping and handling stage, resulting in more profit for you.

Another valuable use of this technique is to direct your page viewers to your "About Me" page. Use this page to invite prospects to be among the first to hear about your latest items. Set up a simple form and invite them to subscribe to your "update" list.

Keep in touch on a regular basis and continue to grow your list of names and email addresses of those people interested in your kind of specialty merchandise.

Do it right and you could build a list of tremendous value. When you think about it, a list of interested prospects and customers is the greatest asset any business could have. As a serious seller on eBay, it's something you'll want to develop too.


## Get Started Early

From the very beginning, your ad has to work hard to capture the attention and interest of as many potential buyers as you possibly can. Your efforts must begin with your title – starting with the very first word -- and the Gallery Image, as these are the first two elements anyone ever sees.

From your very first word, you've got to strive to grab the attention of every single individual who might be even remotely interested in your specific item. It doesn't matter whether buyers shop using the Search function or by scanning the daily listings in their favorite categories. Some items will grab them by the collar and literally pull them inside while most listings will simply be skimmed and passed over.

The key is to jam enough relevant keywords and provide enough "stop-ability" in your title. It's also important to have a Gallery Image that works in tandem with your title to create interest, intrigue, or curiosity.

To get the best results – you need the largest audience possible. But attracting mere curiosity seekers won't benefit you. You really only want interested candidates who have the capability to buy.

Deliver your big idea early. Get your primary benefit into your title as early as possible – starting with the first word, if possible.

*For example...*

> If you're marketing hypnosis CD's, state the main benefit of each – STOP SMOKING… LOSE WEIGHT… GAIN SELF-CONFIDENCE.

> If you're selling a business opportunity, try – START YOUR OWN BUSINESS, SECOND INCOME, or GET RICH.

> If you're selling a lawn mower, try – LUSH GREEN LAWN or NEIGHBOR ENVY.

The key is to grab attention as early as possible with a succinct summary of a desired benefit.

Work to pull prospects inside. It's long been understood in advertising circles that "free" is a powerful draw. But with the proliferation of unsolicited emails promising the sun and moon for free, its' magical powers have been weakened.

A legitimate 'free offer' can still work. However, the key distinction is that it must be legitimate and it must appear so. Free Shipping works well on eBay. Hey, who doesn't like to save a few bucks when they can? We're wired to look for the best value. When one choice offers free shipping and the other one doesn't the one with the freebie usually gets the nod – assuming of course that all else is equal.

Anything that adds unique value to your offer should be mentioned in the title. You've only got 55 characters and you need to make it as compelling as possible while delivering the most significant information.

Suppose you had a collectible figurine from the 1950's. When you opened the retrieved item from your basement storage area, you happened upon a 1950's catalog promoting the entire line at the same time. It would make good sense to offer the catalog in addition to the item. Why? Because the catalog adds value and helps legitimize your offer. But instead of simply stating "catalog included", try something like FREE INTERESTING 1954 GUIDE. That may be a little wordy to stuff into your title, but take note of the concept at work and apply it where you can. This beats simply stating "catalog included".

Success on eBay is all about providing what people want to buy and then giving them reasons to pursue your item.

Your entire listing also needs to provoke positive feelings about you, as though you're well-versed in serving customers, offer exactly what you say you do and you'll ship in a timely manner. Interested prospects do want your item. But they also want to be reassured that they'll get exactly what they think they'll get – or more.

Prospective buyers need to feel good about doing business with you. Your overall listing and presence on eBay conveys information about you, indirectly. This tips people off as to who they're really dealing with. What do your ads say about you? Ideally, you'll be businesslike, with a close personal touch and a willingness to serve. Remember, it's not just the item you're selling here -- you're also selling yourself.

## Provide Enough Information

Give as many relevant details about your items as possible. It's impossible to provide too much factual information, so stack one important detail on top of another and prioritize these in order of importance to the buyer. Every prospect will get their fill to varying degrees. One sales point will sway one buyer to step forward and bid while another will be moved by something else entirely. You never know which key detail will result in that "got to have it" feeling which can trigger a bidding frenzy and an avalanche of profits for you. Best thing to do is include all you can.

Your mission is to get prospects to...

　　1) Use the Buy-It-Now to win the auction...

　　2) Place a bid…

　　3) Leave their email address by signing up to your list so
　　you can let them know about your other related items and
　　hopefully sell them something down the road....

　　4) Mark your auction as one to watch so they'll hopefully
　　return and bid later.

Any other result doesn't count. It doesn't matter if they mark your
auction as one to watch if they don't get in on the action at some
point in time. And it doesn't matter how many page views you
receive. Action in the form of bidding and buying is where it's at
and it's your job as seller to do everything in your power to
encourage more people viewing your page to get in on it before it's
gone for good.

Trigger some kind of action -- even if it's just a question.
Questions should be welcomed by sellers, rather than seen as an
annoyance. If a potential buyer takes the time to ask a question,
they're usually seriously interested in taking the next step. Often a
question will tip you off to a detail you perhaps should have
included in your listing, but somehow overlooked. For the buyer, it
says a lot about you and whether you make the grade.

Questions give you an opportunity to shine in the customer service
area. Always respond promptly, professionally and in a friendly
manner – even to the "stupid" questions that you've already
answered in your description.

You have the option of making any question and answer visible to
all. This means it's a glorious opportunity to let your personality
and professionalism as a seller shine.

Another great advantage is that questions can be answered and made public right up until the close of any auction. This allows you to provide important information to prospective buyers, right up until the last minute. It's a great advantage to be able to so on auctions where you've already received bids. You can always change your descriptions up to the final 12 hours of your listing, as long as there are no bids. But once a bid has been received, you cannot go in and change your description. But you can answer any question, and in so doing, provide important information or clarification.

Balance is important. You should provide just as much detailed information as needed to maximize earnings. The more detail you provide, the more likely it is you'll hook the interest of a larger audience. And the more enticing you can make your ad copy, the more money these people will be willing to bid.

The key consideration on the part of the advertiser (you) is this: Is it worth the investment of time required to add the additional details? That's the balance you need to weigh before exhausting an irreplaceable resource – your time.

Your answer really depends upon the item and the market. If you've picked up some quality collectibles, pieces of jewelry, or rare artifacts from an estate sale, it's likely worth your time to describe each in detail. If you're selling dollar-store merchandise, it's probably not worth your time to elaborate on specific features and benefits in your copy, even though doing so would most likely improve your profits. The reason is that the overall payoff may not be worth the investment.

It really depends on the value you place on your time and how much you can reasonably expect to earn from the sale of that particular item. If you've got a pallet loaded with identical items, by all means, provide all the details you can. You only have to write your ad once, yet you can profit from that single effort hundreds of times over.

## Setting Yourself Up For Success

Here's a secret to getting the most out of every eBay listing: Write your description as though no picture of your item existed.

Let me repeat that again in case you missed it. Write your eBay listing as though you had no picture whatsoever to accompany your description. Yes, photos are a significant part of the eBay success formula, but you'll write better descriptions when you don't rely on your photo as a crutch.

Find a quiet place, get yourself into a relaxed state and clear your mind of any chatter. Now set out to describe your item in as much detail as you can in the reasonable amount of time you've set aside.

A few minutes of focused effort can often do the trick for relatively small, everyday items. If your item is particularly valuable, you can afford to spend more time at this than if you're selling an everyday item. The point of this is to spit out the words and phrases that paint a clear picture of what it is that you're offering.

You can simply take notes or record your thoughts on a tape or digital recorder. Recorders are excellent as you can really get into it without fear of missing something. When you're forced to write it all down the stream of consciousness thinking you've entered into is sometimes forced to take a detour.

When you can devote just a few minutes of concentrated effort to describing a single item, you'll have all the most important bases covered. But there's another benefit to this process that goes beyond simply detailing a product's important characteristics. When you examine the smallest of details, additional benefits you never considered before will jump right out at you. Since benefits are so important in raising the emotional state of the prospect, you're fueling desire and increasing your chances of a bid or an immediate sale.

At first glance, you see only the feature. For example, there's the Velcro strap designed to hold a laptop secure in its case. A novice might mention this in their laptop bag listing, but probably wouldn't expand on it. But with this information fresh in mind, you'll be on the lookout for something more. Perhaps that Velcro strip is triple-stitched for longer life, or it's twice as wide as the standard strap to ensure a tighter hold, so the buyer can rest assured that her valuable machine is safe and secure in transport. Which description is more enticing to you?

It doesn't take much to look beyond the obvious. But most sellers never do. But by doing this simple exercise and describing your item as though a photograph never existed, you'll uncover additional artillery, giving you much more leverage in the marketplace.

It's important to note that the benefits you unearth must be valid benefits. You can't simply create an advantage if it's not perceived as an advantage by your audience. Ideally you want accurate information that triggers desire. The more desirable your descriptions, the more you help potential buyers convince themselves that this is exactly what they need to solve their troubling problem, or to simply make them feel better in some way.

### Think "Classifieds" First – Here's Why

Classified are condensed ads. They're short and sweet. Rarely will you see a classified ad that's more than one paragraph in length. And you don't need any experience to write a few lines about something you want to sell.

Prior to eBay, classified advertising was one of the most popular ways to tell others about that fine item you had available.

Thankfully with eBay, those days have pretty much gone. But not because writing a classified ad was difficult (it's not), but because it was much more expensive to advertise this way and in most cases, you would only reach an audience limited for the most part by geography.

A basic classified ad requires few words... and a well-written one can give you tremendous leverage, making each individual word worth its weight in gold. In my book, *Classified Magic*, I broke down classified advertising to these 3 crucial components:

**1: The Headline...**

**2: The Offer... and...**

**3: The Call to Action and Contact Information.**

All it takes is a handful of words. But in this compact piece of advertising copy, you need to deliver the item's major advantage (headline)... provide a key detail or two (sub-heading)... deliver an appealing reason to buy (offer)... and a directive to action to motivate people to get off the couch and actually do something.

There's a major difference between a classified ad and your eBay listing, however. The difference is that with a classified, you're usually paying for space by the word or line of copy, so economizing on your communication is often essential, to make your ad more affordable. But on eBay, there's no such limitation. You can make you ad as big or as long as you want. And you can write even a condensed ad by using complete, coherent sentences.

So why even consider the classified advertising approach then?

Classifieds are easy -- even for non-writers. Just give yourself a few lines of space and craft the most attractive ad you can muster. You probably won't use this as an actual eBay listing, but in just minutes, you could be off to a roaring start.

Here are a few points to keep in mind:

**1. Focus on the key information about your item.** Start by listing the important details like brand, model, size, color, age, condition, packaging, etc.

**2. Make it sound appealing.** Notice how items offered on the menu of any decent restaurant sound interesting, elegant, and mouthwateringly delicious? Here are a few examples...

> *"Tender Hearts of Fresh, Long Island Scallops Delicately Sautéed in a Garlic Butter and Parmesan-Reggiano Sauce To a Gentle, Golden Brown"*

> *"Freshly-Grilled Portabella Mushrooms Served On a Colorful Medley of Stir Fried Vegetables Handpicked From Our Own Gardens"*

> *"Delicious Chick Peas and Scallions Delicately Prepared in Mama's Own Taste-Tingling, Spicy Curry Sauce, and Served atop Fluffy White Rice"*

Simply apply the same kind of flair to your eBay ads. Make your everyday items sizzle with appeal. Encourage an appetite for your offering.

**3. Focus on the best 1-3 unique advantages or benefits your item offers.** Deliver your best, most provocative and powerful punch right out of the gate. Follow this with another one or two, if you can.

**4. Create an offer.** Your best offer is never just the product alone. Add something to the package – special reports, spare parts, instruction manual or DVD, original packaging, carrying case, or 30-days of email/phone support for your software program. Do so and collectively you'll be offering something of greater value than the product alone could ever deliver.

**5. Trigger action.** Human nature means that most people, interested as they may be in your item, still need a nudge to actually take a positive step forward. Remind them to bid now, or to use your Buy-It-Now option to grab it while it's still available. Scarcity is a huge motivator to action, but most prospects need to be reminded and lead into action.

If you included all of these steps, you'd probably have much more than a simple classified ad. And you won't have to reduce it to fit your ad budget. Each point included could be used 'as is', or enhanced for greater power within your ad description.

But setting out to write nothing more than a tiny classified ad can set you on your way. It's less daunting and easily accomplished in minutes. It may be all you need, or it could give you a huge edge and a terrific start.

## The Half-Page Ad

With this listing format, you simply expand on the key details into a few paragraphs. If you identified 3 major benefits your item offers, take each and write a paragraph detailing what the benefit is, what makes it unique, and why it's something the buyer should take great interest in. Typically, 4-6 paragraphs are all you need to sell many copies of numerous items. The idea is to make it interesting and easy to read and most importantly, compel prospects to action.

An easy way to understand this method is to think of the auction listing you're writing as a small display ad in the newspaper. You've got only a limited time and space to make a compelling argument in favor of action. Follow a proven format and you'll stand a much better chance of getting the kind of response you want. But that means ignoring most of the display ads you see on a daily basis.

To write an effective half-page ad, just remember the old advertising formula that's stood the test of time -- A.I.D.A. *(Attention, Interest, Desire and Action.)*

Your first point of contact needs to quickly capture attention. That's the job of the Title. But once prospects click-through for your full description, your ad has to work hard to keep them reading. So start with a headline.

You can expand on your Title, or craft a separate headline altogether. But the trick is to reinforce the thought that they are indeed on the right page.

Now take that attention and build interest. Here's where those unique benefits come in handy. Stack one on top of the other so a mild interest in your item soon turns to a burning desire to have it.

Then, your job is to guide them down the right path, where that desire is easily met. You've got to get them to follow through and buy now or bid. If you don't accomplish this natural conclusion, the rest of your efforts don't mean a thing.

Your "Half-Page" Ad Model might look something like this...

> Paragraph One: Headline
>
> Paragraph Two: Description of Benefit One
>
> Paragraph Three: Description of Benefit Two
>
> Paragraph Four: Description of Benefit Three
>
> Paragraph Five: Summary of Offer

Paragraph Six: Call To Action


*Or perhaps this…*

Paragraph One:  Big Bold, Benefit-Oriented Headline

Paragraphs Two to Four: An Interesting Story About the Item

Paragraph Five: Call To Action


That's just two examples of what you could do with the half-page technique. You may choose something entirely different and that's fine too. The point is to free your mind of any pressure to create an ad that sells, and just let your selling points flow – one after another.

As a general guideline for many everyday items, all you need is half a page of text. And anybody can write at least half a page in 5 minutes time. Just talk about those things that are most important to your prospect. What makes your item valuable, special, unique, helpful, or a worthwhile purchase or investment? Whatever it is... that's exactly what you need to bring to the forefront.

Below is a short ad that fits the "half-page" format and does an effective job of selling. The underlying concept here would probably work very well on eBay today, although it appeared in the early 1970's book, *The Lazy Man's Way To Riches* by Joe Karbo.

Notice its simplicity and charm. It's written in a matter-of-fact style and justifies the low price offered a couple of different ways. You may not have this kind of opportunity to offer such value, but anyone can certainly learn how to write a simple but powerful eBay ad by studying this example alone.

Try emulating Joe's style. It's a conversational approach – perfect for the eBay marketplace. State your offer and tell why it's such an amazing deal. Make it easy for your prospect to act and build believability into your presentation.

*I have a new Cadillac that I've got to sell because I'm leaving for the Service, next week. It cost me $8,000 and only has 732 miles on it. Rather than sell it to some thief of a car dealer or going to the trouble of advertising, I'll let you have it for $4,000.*

*If you don't have the cash, don't worry about it because I only owe the $4,000 and you can take over my payments (which are about $75 a month).*

*You know I drive carefully, but I'd feel better if you had your mechanic check it out before you buy. In fact, if you'd like to drive it for a couple of days, I'll be glad to deliver it to you with a full tank of gas. And if you don't like the car, I'll take it back and you've had a free ride. No obligation.*

*One thing - it's an awful green color (but you could have it painted).*

*If you're interested, call me at (714) 826-1313 between 7 and 9 tonight.*

You don't have to sell a car to pattern this technique on eBay. Simply tell your story. Introduce what you have to offer buyers in a friendly conversational style and tell them why they should be interested. Make it an exceptional bargain because its actual value will be worth much more to the buyer than the tiny sum you're asking for as a starting bid, or even at the Buy-It-Now price.

Now here's an example of a current ad running on eBay from a successful seller. He's added lots of graphics, but I've only included the text here for our purposes.

*Advanced Broadcast Camera Techniques Videos DVDs Amazing DVD's come with money back guarantee! ADVANCED BROADCAST CAMERA TECHNIQUES Black-Belt Videography 1 & 2 TRAINING VIDEOS - 80 MINS EACH ON 2 DVDS -- Everything You Need To Know To Be a Top Cameraman Or Woman*

*Never before in the history of videography has a video been produced with so much information on advanced camerawork. These DVDs are guaranteed to propel you to the next level - even if you are already an award-winning videographer.*

*Advanced Broadcast Camera Techniques Vol. 1 & 2 reveals over 900 examples of the best camerawork and how to achieve it. Over 100 chapters and 160 minutes of teaching that guarantees to improve your camerawork 50 percent or more or your money back.*

*You may think you are a good cameraperson now, but wait until you watch these videos. You will be shocked by how much you will learn that you are not doing now. Also includes a two-page shot list for you to carry with you to the job. These are the videos everyone is talking about!*

*If you get any videos this year, get these.*
*(4 testimonials here + a link to an independent review)*

*Videos come with a one year free email tech support as well as a money back guarantee. You are sure to pick up some great shots that you are not doing now. You are bidding on a two DVD set. Advanced Broadcast Camera Techniques Volume One and Two 80 minutes each.*

*THIS AUCTION IS FOR 2 ADVANCED BROADCAST CAMERA TECHNIQUES TRAINING TAPES - 80 MINS EACH ON DVD*

Could you write something like this?

Of course you could! In fact, apply as much of what you learn here as you can and your ads could be world-beaters. A few paragraphs may be all you need to quickly create a compelling ad that makes you good money.

An easy way to get started is to place the item within view. Now look at it as a prospect or customer would. List whatever product features jump out at you within the first 60 seconds. Don't struggle to find these features, simply jot down words or phrases that pop into your mind as you examine this particular item.

Now ask yourself what it is about this feature that gives the item value.

Let's suppose you've got a wood carving to sell. So you begin by listing things like its overall size, condition, material it's made from, mounting hardware, and so on. You note that the wood is a rich, orangey-red color. It's an unusual wood, something you just don't see everyday. The specific type isn't yet known, so you do some digging. After a quick check from the supplier, you learn that it's actually made from an exotic species called African Padauk. Turns out it's a rare, handcrafted piece of natural beauty and charm, and not at all like the typical carvings found in local gift shops.

This is precisely the kind of information you want to reveal in your description. It's this kind of detail that can make a huge difference in the profit earned at sale.

Take those features you've identified and transform each into a glowing benefit. As you'll recall, features are always about what the product is and benefits are always about what it does for the customer.

Here's an example of descriptive, benefit-oriented sales copy. Notice how enticing it is. If the author of this piece could make something as ordinary as an everyday pencil sound this inviting, imagine what you can do with the items you plan to sell.

*How To Sell A Second-Hand Pencil That Has No Eraser*

*Forget laundry bills forever! This pre-tested chrome yellow hard-finished writing instrument positively will not leak and keeps your hands free of ink and your clothes safe and spotless.*

*Fabricated from the finest second-growth hickory, it is graphite-filled with fine-grained, jet-black carbon that cannot snag or catch on any paper surface. Oven-baked enamel coating, with die-stamped copper in two-toned filigree. Removal of the erasure guarantees pencil to be 100 percent latex-free.*

*No push-pull, no click-click. The point is always there, ready to write. Free from unsightly pocket clip, it writes in any weather. Funnel-shaped point is handsomely decorated with scalloped edge. Refilling unnecessary; can be discarded when finished. Fits any standard sharpener. Order now.*

Here's a short ad that describes a piece of clothing in an interesting and appealing way.

Contrast this description with most ads offered on eBay and you'll see how this approach automatically raises the perceived value of the item, setting it apart from what some might consider just another piece of clothing.

*Men's First Quality Italian-Made Suit Size 40*

*You're bidding on a piece of luxury. It's a beautiful, black suit, handmade in Italy and brought to Philadelphia by my brother-in-law Roberto, last month. It looks amazing and it feels wonderful to wear.*

*What's most remarkable about it is the quality that's built-in. It's made by hand, which means it takes 3 times longer to craft this beauty than it does the average suit of good-quality. Because of all the extra attention given it, it's likely to last at least 3 times longer too.*

*But the biggest difference between this custom-made treasure and an off-the-rack suit is that its' designer's touch makes it look great on anyone. Seriously, if Roberto can look that good, you will too.*

*The fabric is stunning and soft to the touch. In fact, the tailor says this fabric is the highest grade available anywhere in the world. Imagine... a first-class, handmade designer suit, for less than you'd expect to pay at a cheap warehouse.*

*Bid now and this gorgeous handmade suit could be yours - for far less than you ever imagined.*

## Chapter Three: 3 Easy Ways To Write Powerful eBay Ads in As Little As 5 Minutes

5 Minute Ad -- Method Number One
5-Minute Ad -- Method Number Two
5 Minute Ad -- Method Number Three
Deliver Powerful 'Reasons Why'
Service Today's Short Attention Span

To get you into the right frame of mind, I want to begin with a short sample ad. This particular ad below is just one paragraph long. And I'm here to tell you that anyone can easily write a single paragraph in five minutes. In fact most people can probably write more than that.

It's important that you adopt a selling mindset. In other words, the methods that follow need to be approached from a sales perspective. You're not just writing to be heard. You're writing to actually turn your item into cash.

Here's another example of a short, but effective ad...

*Speed-Reading mastery in 30 days at home. Double your reading speed by day two. Age doesn't matter. If you can read at a basic level, you can quickly increase your speed with this course.*

*It's called Speed Reading Success Secrets and it's a new, improved & updated version of our best-selling program.*

*No expensive CD's to acquire, no home study courses to buy, and no seminars to attend. No boring theory either. Everything is in this one book. You get only what works and the tools you need to make it happen lightning-fast.*

*Easy to learn and use. Devour books, reports, manuals, and courses in far less time. You'll be surprised. Your friends will be shocked.*

*It's already being used by thousands of business owners, doctors, lawyers, scientists, researchers, and college students worldwide. Over 33,400 online customers -- and growing.*

*100% Satisfaction Guaranteed. You must be thrilled - or your money cheerfully refunded.*

## 5 Minute Ad -- Method #1

You could easily model this ad, or create one from scratch. The only catch is... you must not spend any more time on this than five minutes. It's a challenge... but one that will produce some impressive results for you – guaranteed.

Do not guess at the time. Use your pocket timer and set it for five minutes. This is the only way to stay on track and on course. Without a timer, you'll more than likely spend more time than you think. But when you know you've got just a few minutes, it forces your brain to get busy and with a little practice, you'll come up with your best material quickly and almost effortlessly.

Take out an item you'd like to sell on eBay. It can be anything at all. If you don't have an item handy, find something else to use. Next, set your timer and open up a new page in your word processor. Then... go nuts for those five minutes. Capture everything about your item that might make it more interesting, beneficial, and valuable to buyers. Just keep writing for those five minutes. Describe all your product's attributes in an interesting way. Don't look up until the timer sounds.

Did you follow through and do this exercise? If so, terrific! If not, you know what to do.

If you completed this exercise, what kind of results did you get? I bet you're impressed with what you just accomplished in those 5 minutes. And that's with only a little bit of help in terms of direction. What you've just pulled off is Method Number One for writing an effective eBay ad in five minutes.

Now let's provide a little more direction and see how that works.

Place the item in front of you. If it's a small item, put it on the table or chair across from you. If the item is larger, just leave it on the floor.

Now... imagine for a moment, the type of person who would want to buy it. Get a clear picture of your prospect in your mind's eye and become that person. Act as the buyer. Put yourself in their shoes and be willing to play along.

Identify the major motivation for buying the item in question. Most product purchases are driven by emotion. Emotions are a combustible force that influences the decision to buy. Once again, here's the list of the major controlling forces that influences purchasing decisions.

Powerful buying triggers include...

**The need to feel important**

**The desire for better health**

**The yearning for recognition**

**The pride of accomplishment**

**The longing for love**

**The desire for romance/ romantic fulfillment**

**The urge to look attractive/ feel beautiful/ appear more desirable**

**The lust for power**

**The yearning for independence**

**The craving for financial stability**

**The need to feel secure/ salvation**

**The hunger for self esteem/ self-regard**

**The hunger for peer or community recognition**

**The fear of loss**

**The fear of shame**

**The fear of the unknown**

What drives people to buy the type of item you're listing? Harness the underlying force that drives your prospect's behavior and you can get more visitors to bid and send the selling price skyward.

Next, set your timer for 5 minutes. The idea here is to spend 5 minutes – no more, no less – and to use emotional benefits (and any technical details you deem important) to sell your prospect on your item.

You can use any number of angles to convince this individual prospect to bid or buy now. And I want you to approach this as though your very future depended on it. In other words... you simply MUST make the sale – or else!

Hold nothing back. Let your mind work its magic. You can work from your computer and keyboard, or use a pad of paper and a pen.

If you've got an audio recorder, that's even easier as you won't be slowed down by the mechanics of typing or writing and can capture the ideas as fast as you can speak them.

Simply transcribe your recording at the end of the five minutes. After this short interval, you've probably got an interesting and compelling message. It may be in raw, unedited format. But with a little adjusting you're quickly on your way to an ad that sells.


## 5-Minute Ad -- Method #2

Once again, you'll need your trusty timer. At first, you might find this handy little device a little irritating. But after a while, you'll realize just how valuable a tool it is. It forces you to focus on the task at hand and pretty soon, you'll be crafting compelling messages -- in just a few minutes.

*Phase One*

During the first phase of this technique, we're going to start with even less time. 60 seconds is all you have for this preliminary step. But you're not trying to write any ad copy here. You're simply brainstorming and capturing key words related to your item.

Now set your timer to sound after one minute. In those 60 seconds, I want you to jot down 5-7 words, thoughts, or phrases that come to mind that best describe your item.

It's important to put your sales hat on before you begin, and view the item as your prospective buyer would. Whatever words arise, jot them down or speak them into your recorder and transcribe later.

What words best describe the value, advantage, or benefit the lucky buyer is about to obtain? That's what you want to capture at this point, in just a few words. When you hear the timer, stop this exercise.

*Phase Two*

Now quickly review your list and arrange them in order of priority – from the most appealing attribute to the least. You want to always start off with your biggest bang to capture the largest audience and keep them riveted to your message. You should now have a prioritized list of at least 3-5 words or phrases. The next step is to turn each of these into a descriptive paragraph, allowing one minute for each.

*Phase Three*

Set your timer and get ready. The intention here is to explain the benefit or advantage in way that sounds interesting. In other words, explain the benefit clearly and give yourself one minute on each. Expand on each word or thought you just brainstormed so that it makes sense and appeals to the target audience.

*Phase Four*

After writing a short paragraph for each, it's time to assess what you've got and make any necessary changes. Polish it up for maximum impact. Your objective in any ad writing process is to write a description that sells in every sentence. Here's a secret: Whenever you're stuck for what to say next, simply preface it with the words "You get".

> *You get a Red Flyer wagon that's in excellent, refurbished condition, re-built the original way using top-quality made-in-America parts, not the cheap imported components that almost look the same but won't last half as long.*

See how easy it is? Good. Now here's how you can enhance the "You get" solution even further. After utilizing the first element –

"You get", you simply add a follow-up such as "so that" or "which means" or even "therefore".

> *"You get 4 shiny new rubber wheels with solid steel cores **so that** your refurbished wagon looks just like the original Red Flyer... PLUS it's sure to last much longer than most new wagons on the market today.*

If you haven't covered the big payoff or benefit with the first segment, the second will help you bring it forth in a way that sounds quite natural.

Use this technique and it will help channel your thinking and keep you focused on the item from your potential buyer's perspective.

## 5 Minute Ad -- Method #3

Take a list of keywords related to your item. You can use the words already collected from your headline brainstorming session, or simply take a minute to create a list now.

The purpose of brainstorming is to generate unfiltered ideas by opening up the creative part of your brain. Just let the ideas flow, unencumbered. Don't judge or analyze. For the set period of time (in this case, one minute) simply allow the ideas or words to come out. Be sure to record them all -- no matter how whacky or unqualified an idea may at first appear.

When you follow this technique, you'll quickly create more data than you'll likely use. But that's a good thing because you get to pick out only the best words and ideas to use in your ad.

Now choose 5 words or phrases that could easily be a great match for your product. For example, the previous ad for the speed reading course might have been created from a list of words like this...

New
30 Days
Double Speed
Anyone
Guaranteed
Practical
All-Inclusive

Next, set your timer for one minute. Now take one word at a time and write a paragraph about it. Take the first word on your list and expand it into something more descriptive and meaningful. You don't just want to make a bold claim... you want to prove that what you say is true.

If your product is "new" how can you expand on that? That's easy. Simply explain that what the buyer gets is brand new, direct from the distributor in its original sealed, box. That's a little more descriptive than simply stating that the item is "new". An accompanying photograph that clearly shows the sealed package acts as visual proof. There's congruency to your words.

At the end of five minutes, you should have 5 different paragraphs pertaining to exactly what it is you're offering. But instead of 5 boring lines about your item, you've got important, value-laden benefits and details that are sure to keep genuine prospects interested, engaged and ready to buy.

You now know a few different ways to create an ad that sells in as little as 5 minutes. It's not exactly rocket science – anyone can do this. It takes some effort... but the rewards are worth it.

The more ads you write, the easier it will come to you. But simply follow these guidelines and you'll get maximum advertising leverage in minimum time.

Here are the keys to creating powerful Item Descriptions in as little as 5 minutes:

- *Make everything you say or write be of useful benefit to the prospective buyer*

- *Get the reader involved emotionally by understanding the underlying reasons for buying*

- *Shape your benefits to feed the predominant reason for buying*

- *Make the results you suggest not only possible to attain but reachable by anyone who follows the simple directions included*

- *Make yourself credible by providing proof and by developing a stellar reputation with a strong Feedback rating*

- *Use your Gallery Image and Title to command the attention of an interested audience*

- *Make what is being offered worth much more than the asking bid so prospects see that it's worth fighting for*

Use these 5-minute solutions and you'll leverage your time and effort. As a result, you'll create listings that communicate with the target buyer in a way that matters -- producing superior overall results for you.

Know the specific information that's most important to your buyer. Find value where value never seemed to exist before. Do this and you'll boost desire for your item, while adding to your bank balance at the same time.

## Deliver Powerful 'Reasons Why'

Every effort you exert in writing your ads should be directed towards one desired result – getting action. You want your reader to do at least one of the following, in order of preference:

**1. Choose the Buy-It-Now option at your set price**

**2. Place a bid on your item now**

**3. Come back and place a bid while the listing is still active**

**4. Leave an email address where you can get in touch with the prospect, with his or her permission**

**5. Mark your auction as one to watch with the intention to return**

Those who click on your title and visit your auction listing without doing anything more are of no value to you, the seller. You've got to be business-like in your approach. After all, it does cost you money, even though eBay is about the best moneymaking opportunities ever available.

If your item doesn't sell at a profit, you have to absorb the loss. So everything you say and do should ultimately lead the reader/prospect to an action immediately.

Sure, most bids don't happen right away as many experienced buyers prefer to wait for those last minute bidding frenzies. But the overall objective of each listing is to make the sale and net a healthy profit. That way, you can go out and do it again and again. Strive to make every paragraph, every sentence, even every word, present your item in the most enticing way possible.

Don't hesitate to tell your prospects precisely why they should bid now. They're obviously interested or they wouldn't spend more than a few seconds visiting your listing. Remind them that it's easy to put it off until later -- and then miss out entirely. Surely that's something they don't want to let happen. Buying now gives them what they want at a great price. Bidding now keeps them in the game -- at least for the time being.

Provide reasons why visitors should buy from you. Many items listed week by week have numerous direct competitors on eBay. With a little searching, buyers can easily find this out for themselves. Now they have choices and your ad might be just one of many.

Be sure to emphasize your positive track record and remind people of your nearly perfect Feedback rating. Let them know exactly what they can expect from you. It's one thing to say it, but something else entirely to follow through on your promises with consistency.

Answer all questions as soon as they're posted. Provide accurate information and project a friendly, good-to-to-business-with-you attitude. Eliminate any reason NOT to buy from you.

Set yourself apart in the service and product delivery areas and make yourself available to others. If you screw up, admit it, resolve the situation and move on.

Nobody's perfect. Sometimes things happen. Packages get damaged despite your elaborate packaging job. Others are misplaced. Answers sometimes are delayed. And descriptions can be misunderstood and interpreted as something else entirely. Don't run from the situation. Don't ignore emails from other eBay members. Face up to it and deal with it as best you can. In the long run, that's always the best way to handle any such incidents.

Stress what's even a little bit different about your product versus another your prospects could stumble upon. Give them clear reasons why your item is a better choice. Paint a colorful picture of all that's included in the offer and present it as a package that's clearly worth more to the buyer than the basic product from an unknown seller who probably doesn't go to the same extent you do to serve customers and ensure their satisfaction.

## Service Today's Short Attention Span

Never before in the history of the world has the average consumer had such an abundance of choice. Everywhere you look, and even where you don't, it seems as though there's an unlimited smorgasbord of choice. This means there's always something competing for your prospects attention. Diversion is available at every turn.

The solution is to write tight copy. Make every sentence pay its own freight. The short speed reading ad is an example of making every word pay. In other words, enhance the meaning of your message by directing it towards your potential bidder. Make it all about what they get out of the deal. And that's never just a product, but a positive experience of some kind.

Whatever you offer should be presented as something that's as advantageous to the buyer as possible. Stack as many benefits into your copy as you can justify (keeping time constraints in mind) and make them more enticing... more sizzling... and more irresistible.

A genuine benefit is always worth learning about to a true prospect. And always emphasize your quality of service as indicated by your Feedback rating and documented by the comments inside.

# Chapter Four: Why People Buy on eBay and How To Use This Information To Increase Your Profits

Buyers Enjoy an Unlimited Variety & Selection
Bargain Hunters Seek and Often Find Discount Prices
eBay Offers The Ultimate in Convenience
Buying on eBay is Still a Novelty
Buyers Love The Unique Shopping Experience eBay Provides
It's Safe and Secure Here
It's a Fun, Competitive Environment That Gets People Involved
eBay Offers Reliability

I've included this chapter because it's important to understand what it is that pulls millions of buyers to eBay. Everyone has their own reasons and I've featured several of the most predominant ones below.

If you want to make a lot of money selling on eBay, it's important to tap into the mindset of those you hope to reach and persuade. The more you understand what people want -- the better you'll be able to provide it.

## Buyers Enjoy an Unlimited Variety & Selection

There are very few items that can't be found on eBay in any given month. If you conduct a search this week and can't find exactly what you're looking for, chances are it will appear in the following week or two.

If you can imagine it, you can find it on eBay – as long as it's legal and doesn't contravene eBay policy. Recently eBay has promoted this fact with their "It" campaign. Whatever "It" is… you can find "it" on eBay. Astute shoppers know this already and often go to eBay as their first – if not only – option.

You can find high quality merchandise and bargain-basement items too. Any brand name you can think of can be found in its corresponding category. Unique and unusual items you just don't see in even the most specialized retail shops tend to show up on eBay on a regular basis. Even extremely rare pieces, autographed items, artifacts, and celebrity memorabilia appear on eBay – rather than at those well-established auction houses that have existed for a hundred years or more.

In short, eBay delivers an unending supply of products of various shapes, sizes, and values. Buyers can locate items and discover new, interesting products that are simply unavailable anywhere else in the world. It's a one-of-a-kind marketplace that's changed the shopping habits of millions of people.

Currently there are more than 40,000 different categories of items on eBay and many of those categories have thousands and thousands of individual listings. Every day the inventory changes as items are sold or listings expire.

Only eBay provides such a vast diversity of items available through one channel. You can buy brand new products in the same perfect condition you'd find at a retailer. You can find items that haven't been sold on the open market for 30 or 40 years... yet they're still in mint condition with original packaging, preserved by pack-rat collectors all over the globe. And it's only eBay where you can find a product -- in whole or in part.

Yes, you can get parts, pieces, re-built components, refurbished, even specialized packaging materials to suit any of the above. You can buy singles, doubles or complete sets. For example, you could find a John Deere tractor – new or used – or a single replacement wheel for that same tractor.

eBay is the one place in the whole world where nothing is permanently unavailable. With such a variety of choice, it's no wonder eBay has become the number one choice for millions of buyers. And it keeps growing larger every day -- which is good news for you.

## Bargain Hunters Seek and Often Find Discount Prices

Everybody loves a bargain and due to its vast size, eBay offers more bargains than just about any other venue. Not only can buyers find anything they want, they can also discover some outstanding deals too.

Locating, bidding on, and then winning a wanted item at a great price is an exhilarating experience for anyone. For the serial shopper, it's euphoric.

The desire for bargains is a fundamental human trait. Few will willingly spend more money than is necessary to get what they want. But interestingly, they'll often fight until the bitter end to come out on top at the end of the auction. It's what makes us human and it's what makes eBay one of the most successful businesses ever created anywhere on the planet.

Attractive pricing draws attention. It's this magnetic pulling power that inevitably leads to bids. The more bids each listing attracts, the higher the price climbs and the more money you earn as the seller. So, one of the keys to higher profits is to start your auctions at prices that are low enough to raise the eyebrows of the largest number of prospective customers.

Getting maximum attention is primary to earning maximum profits. Since humans are built to automatically favor a lower price, that's exactly what you should offer -- most of the time. The lower the starting price relative to the value of the item, the more tempting and alluring it becomes. A lower price widens the net of prospects, luring more of them into your listing.

Bargain prices are difficult to ignore. So if you've got an in-demand product, a great description and photograph, combined with an opening bid that's going to catch the attention of even the less active shoppers among us, you've got a solid foundation for an appealing eBay ad.

The only downside (and this could be a serious problem) is when your item sells at a ridiculously low price, cutting your margins to the bare bone, or worse, costing you money. Yes, it does happen, though most sellers don't like to talk about it much. But you can relax. This entire publication is designed to help you make maximum money with effective listings that sell. If you stick to these principles, you'll quickly become a more successful seller.

As the ultimate source for low cost merchandise, eBay is the first place many prospective buyers look. eBay is well known as the place to locate all kinds of wonderful things to suit every desire – at a substantial discount. If they can't find it on eBay, chances are they won't find it locally either – even in the largest cities in the world.

Even if it is available locally, there's always a reasonable chance to get a comparable product at a discount on eBay.

Essentially the magic of eBay is that the prospective buyer gets to be part of the negotiation. No longer is the "suggested retail price" the only option, as it often is elsewhere. Even merchandise marked "on sale" means that the sticker price is usually the only acceptable price the merchant will accept. But this all changes radically on eBay.

Unlimited options make retail prices less of a factor to prospects. They can often save money on new, refurbished, used, or "as-is" merchandise, so the price the local store charges doesn't matter much. Here they can choose the option that meets their needs while providing good value.

## eBay Offers The Ultimate in Convenience

As the world's greatest super-mall, eBay never closes. All any consumer could ever want, or imagine wanting is probably available on eBay as you're reading these words.

But you don't have to get yourself prepared, start the car and then begin take a lengthy journey just to arrive. eBay is right at your fingertips, anytime of day or night, and you don't even have to be dressed to happily shop until you've had your fill. All you need is a computer and a basic internet connection and you have immediate access to literally millions of different items divided by category for organizational purposes.

The internet has revolutionized consumer shopping. But it's eBay that's taken the concept to the highest degree. It's catalog shopping from home. But the catalog provided is more like the entire Encyclopedia Britannica sitting on your bookshelf. And rather than sorting through multiple volumes, eBay's simple Search Tool makes it a breeze for consumers to narrow their search and find an exact match in only a few seconds.

eBay saves people time and spares them the pressures of trying to locate that perfect gift. It relieves the anxiety of finding a nearby parking spot at the mall and trying to make it inside before the stores close for the evening. All anyone has to do is just enter a search term and click away. Instantly all relative items appear in sequence and the user can arrange those listings to best match his or her needs and wants.

On eBay, the power is in the hands of the consumer. It's quick and easy to comparison shop for many items. Shoppers often have the choice of bidding on open auctions or buying instantly at a fixed price. Even those with extremely hectic schedules can still find time to browse, bid, and buy on eBay.

It's instantly accessible 24 hours a day, every day of the year. Scores of shoppers are active on eBay at any time, every day of the week. Buyers can locate and acquire your items from home, at work, in their hotel rooms, at "hot-spots" like Starbucks, mall kiosks – even hospital lobbies and libraries.

You never know where on the planet your next buyer resides, or precisely when they'll buy. It could happen anywhere, at any time of day or night. For any entrepreneur or business, eBay is the quickest way to reach a market, whether what you're offering is brand new and direct from the factory, or has been passed along through the hands of a dozen individual owners.

## Buying on eBay is Still a Novelty For Many

eBay has been around in some form since 1995. Today's version is dramatically different from those early days, though the foundational principles of fair trade set forth by founder, Pierre Omidyar, are a big part of eBay's raging success. It's fair to say that eBay's growth and evolution has been nothing short of revolutionary.

eBay is hugely popular on a global scale. It's cool to "eBay" at virtually any age. With its simple interface and quick accessibility, "eBaying" is grade-school easy, even for those among us who didn't exactly grow up with computers.

It's fast becoming a dominant force in trade and commerce. eBay has evolved as a key tool in the way people exchange goods and services. It's an ever-changing inventory and a global marketplace that has revolutionized the way many of us buy and sell things.

eBay is so radically different from anything before that it appeals to a wide cross section of people. It's fun, exciting and highly addictive.

Once you've received your purchased item and it's exactly what you wanted, it's almost impossible to resist the temptation to go back and do the same thing again and buy some more. This is especially true when the item you've now acquired is hard to find anywhere else, or you managed to get it at a great price.

Media types love eBay. They feed off the bizarre, high-profile items as word spreads of these types of new listings. If Oprah Winfrey or Elton John donates an item to charity, it's usually listed on eBay. When that happens, word spreads through so many different media outlets that it's almost impossible not to hear about it.

You'd have to be living in a cave to have missed some of the whacky auctions and the high prices paid to winning bidders. I'm talking about items like the half-eaten grilled cheese sandwich that apparently featured an image of the Virgin Mary and sold for a whopping $24,000… or the guy who sold his ex-wife's wedding dress for 3,850 pounds -- by modeling the dress himself.

There's no doubt that the impact of the media has played a significant role and helped to fuel the exponential growth of eBay.

One of the things that caught my attention and heightened my interest was a story I heard on a local news channel in Toronto. It was about this woman who had found a potato chip from a freshly opened bag that seemed quite unique. No, it wasn't anything disgusting at all. Instead, this chip featured a cutout in the shape of a star.

This smart Seller seized the opportunity and put it aside, rather than eating it and then later listed this single potato chip on eBay. It sold about a week later for something like $250US. What this story did was awaken me to the possibilities on eBay. It also had an immediate impact on my snacking habits.

## Buyers Love The Unique Shopping Experience eBay Provides

Browsing and buying on eBay is radically different from any other shopping experience. It represents an unlimited shopping environment for consumers – one that they control. For the seller, it's the ultimate free-enterprise opportunity. Anyone, anywhere can market globally from the corner of their garage or basement.

Here it's the customer who sets the price – not the retailer. It's a refreshing change in the way the customer gets to buy. Only offline auctions presented this kind of buying freedom before. But such auctions have always been limited in number, in the kinds of things available for purchase, and in the frequency and accessibility of such events.

Now the buyer is central to each sale. A seller exhibits an item in the hope of generating a sale and earning a profit. The prospective buyer gets to examine it, even though the item could be thousands of miles away. He or she can ask questions about any listing and decide whether to bid (or use the Buy-It-Now option, when available) based on the responses received and the overall gut-level feeling about the seller and the sales proposition.

Great deals are scooped up every day on eBay leaving happy buyers delirious with joy. Other auctions close at prices well above what the seller might have only dreamed about earlier.

For the prospective buyer, the opportunity for a fabulous buy intrigues and invites action. Interested buyers get to offer only as much as they're willing to spend. This makes previously unattainable items within reach. But it also invites others to take a crack at it. With few other bids, prices often remain low, whereas lots of action usually means a spike in the selling price.

It's this kind of price freedom that attracts millions of buyers from around the globe. Interested shoppers submit the amount they're willing to pay. If it meets the buyer's minimum and no one else bids, it's theirs.

With competitive bids in play, it's the active participants – the bidders themselves -- who get to decide how much they really want it and vary their bids accordingly. The price listed at the close of the auction is the point of agreement between buyer and seller – and that's where the sales transaction takes place.

What really turns buyers on to eBay is the speed at which they can find the item they're looking for. It's a super-fast way to locate almost any item for sale. You can find whatever you want in mere moments from the comfort of your easy chair, whenever and wherever the idea strikes. It's a radical departure from traditional shopping at even the most successful, large-scale retailers like Staples, Home Depot, or Walmart.

## It's Safe and Secure Here

Although no business environment or system is 100% foolproof, eBay is a safe and secure place to do business across the country, or around the world. The checks and balances eBay has implemented, helps to keep problems to a minimum.

You sell to other "members" – which means they've gone through the brief registration process. Does this prevent undesirable characters from getting in? No it doesn't -- at least not entirely. But in my experience, eBay is a microcosm of society itself. 99.9% of the people here are decent, honest individuals who keep the wheels of eBay turning smoothly with commitments that stick and transactions that benefit both buyer and seller.

Occasionally, a bad apple gets into the barrel. In my 4+ years on eBay and after several hundred transactions, I've had two encounters with less than honest people. As a percentage, it's miniscule. So I choose to focus on the overwhelming majority of transactions that go through without a hitch.

If you do enough business (in any type of setting, not just eBay) you will occasionally encounter frauds, fakes, and general nuisances. But if let them stop you, the bad guys win.

Just run a tight ship and be upfront and fair with people and you'll have many more successful transactions than the ones that go sour. If when you do run into a problem, be sure to utilize the resources that are available to you through eBay.

You can significantly increase your chances of success by clearly stating – even restating – your terms and conditions of the sale. Seller's who succinctly state things like how quickly they'll ship upon receiving payment, methods of payment accepted, exact amounts for shipping and handling to specific areas and the like, go a long way towards building a safe and secure mindset among prospects.

Obviously it's in eBay's best interest to weed out the nut cases and help ensure safe, secure, and smooth trading for everyone. They encourage potential customers to "Buy Safely" and to "Check the Seller's Reputation" before placing a bid.

Feedback is a wonderful tool for doing just that. Most buyers know that you can get a pretty good handle on what someone's like to do business with by scrolling through a couple of windows worth of feedback.

Still, every transaction does involve some risk. This is true in any method of buying, whether it's retail, door-to-door, by mail, or online from a website. But eBay provides the extra advantage of Feedback to help prospective bidders assess their relative confidence level in dealing with a particular vendor, before they put a nickel on the line.

eBay continues to thrive because the vast majority of auctions are carried out safely and securely. If a first-time buyer is a little hesitant initially, they soon get over it when their merchandise arrives and it's exactly as advertised.

## It's a Fun, Competitive Environment That Gets People Involved

Some people enjoy the thrill of competition. They spot an item they want and decide that they simply *must* have it. For the seller, this is an excellent position to be in. But what you really need is two or more people who deeply desire the item in question. When you activate this kind of intensity and burning desire, logic tends to fall by the wayside.

These buyers will stop at nothing to come out on top. They may second-guess themselves the next day and experience buyer's remorse. But thankfully for sellers everywhere, any bid on eBay is a binding agreement to purchase.

So any buyer has to comply and pay up if they win the item, or risk being banned from the site altogether. Since most people are honest, the majority of these auctions end successfully – meaning the seller does get paid the full purchase price.

It's easy for bidders to get caught up in the excitement of eBay. Often an opening bid is so ridiculously low in contrast to the item's true value that it's difficult not to jump in and bid -- just for the heck of it. There's always the chance of winning the item at this low price, should it fail to attract any other bidders. Many great deals have been had this way. It's all part of the magical allure of eBay.

Some folks just have to win at all costs. On eBay, the winner takes all, while the losers go home empty-handed. This is easy to see and understand after a listing ends where two or more bidders fought it out until the bitter end. But with additional inventory, you can offer the same item to anyone else who bid and at your discretion, allowing you to generate additional revenue from a single listing.

You'd think that if someone went to this extent, they'd gladly accept the product, even if they didn't come out on top. But what I've found through experience is that on these runaway auctions, that's just not the case most of the time.

My feeling is that it was the thrill of competing that kept these bidders in the game. To accept a Second Chance offer is like taking the second place ribbon in the spaghetti eating contest at the county fair. So they lick their wounds and carry on to fight another battle. Winning is everything to these super-competitive people, and settling for less just isn't in their nature.

It's the thrill if bidding and having taken ownership (imaginatively, at least) that gets people excited. When they're suddenly outbid, they fight back. And the only solution is to ultimately bid higher and higher amounts to keep it as their property. It's this head-to-head competition that's challenging, energizing and exciting – and tremendously profitable to the seller.

Serious competitors thrive on the thrill of this often intense, 'back and forth' action. For sellers, it's the ultimate scenario. Multiple prospects vying for the same item triggers even more traffic, higher bids, and ultimately a far higher final selling price.

When emotion takes over, any semblance of logic or rationality quickly vanishes. It's the thrill of the win -- that's what matters. And eBay provides unlimited opportunity to compete and win.

## eBay Offers Reliability

Veteran buyers know how eBay works. As massive, complex, and sophisticated as the eBay machine is, it's also remarkably easy for anyone to use. After a successful transaction and receipt of the appropriate merchandise, it's completely irresistible for most people to go back and find some more interesting items.

Smart sellers cater to the wishes of the marketplace. They know the importance of timely responses, careful packaging, and prompt shipping. As a result, they attract even more positive feedback, which in turn makes them appear more trustworthy and reputable to new customers.

Repeat eBay buyers recognize eBay as an incredible source of unlimited merchandise and great value. Essentially eBay is a cost-effective way to catalog and make available unlimited quantities of products from the world's stores, warehouses, liquidation centers, craftspeople, authors, software developers, attics, garages, basements, libraries, and more.

It's a treasure trove of everything under the sun. But users don't have to sift through racks of merchandise, or take a distant trip at a scheduled time to personally attend an auction. It's all there, right at their fingertips… and it's accessible at any hour, from any location.

eBay is a brilliant solution that has and will continue to revolutionize modern society as we know it. It's catalog shopping – without the catalog. Only eBay gives you round the clock buying power with an ever-growing and changing inventory of products, specialty items, collectibles, and services.

You can zero in on exactly what you're looking for in seconds. eBay helps you find anything fast – wherever it may happen to be on the planet. Buyers know it. That's one of the reasons why they come back again and again.

# Chapter Five: How To Sell Any Product, Anytime on eBay

The One Sales Secret That Can Explode Your Results
Understanding Basic Human Desires
Facilitate Buying
Get To Know Your Potential Customers
Learn From Your Competitors
Simple Keys To Successful eBay Selling
Do It Differently
Use Stories

## The One Sales Secret That Can Explode Your Results

People buy emotionally and justify their purchases logically -- after the fact. This one truth holds up in any sales arena, including eBay, and for the vast majority of purchases. Accepting this as fact and learning how to apply it to your listings can make a huge difference in your results, not just today but for as long as you remain an active merchant of goods or services.

Emotions drive almost every buying decision. If someone doesn't *want* a particular item, it doesn't matter how much they *need* it. They simply won't buy. Yet most of us tend to think we buy for logical reasons, and we cling to any shred of evidence to prove it. With a strong desire for a particular item, sound reasoning to the contrary falls by the wayside.

As humans, we're emotional creatures. We think, decide, and take actions based on our emotions. How your potential customer feels at the moment of truth determines what action he or she takes. Present your case in a way that satisfies emotionally -- and you're well on your way to creating a desire for ownership, thus increasing your chances of a bid or instant sale.

When the 'want' is strong enough, most people will move mountains to get it. Nothing can get in the way of the buyer who has set their sights on your item and is determined to not allow it slip from their grasp.

Selling on eBay in some ways is like selling anywhere else. Give people what they want. Allow them to gain the emotional satisfaction of ownership in their minds before the transaction actually transpires. Link the positive emotions they want to experience to your product. Evoke feelings of newfound pleasure, pride of ownership, and promised rewards that can be attained with your item. That's how top salespeople and direct marketers sell.

Help your interested prospects to see themselves with the prize at the end of your auction. It's not so much the new set of Calloway golf clubs… but what it will mean to their game and how that will make them feel about themselves as a result. The real reward is the emotional payoff that can only be theirs to experience if they win.

Allow prospects to figuratively take ownership of your item. Let them feel what it would mean on a deeper level. They need to see themselves enjoying the benefits and they need to feel the wonderful feelings that go along with it.

The greater the intensity and value of those feelings, the stronger the desire to attain them and the more money your buyers will happily spend to gain those deep-seated cravings.

If they can't emotionalize the advantages, they simply won't buy. Get readers to feel the benefits your item offers to a greater degree and you're profits will rise by default.


## Understanding Basic Human Desires

What drives your prospective buyer? What is the underlying force that nudges him to buy your item? According to genius marketer and one of the world's highest paid copywriters, Gary Bencivenga,

*"Emotions are the fire of human motivation, the combustible force that secretly drives most decisions to buy."*

The vast majority of products are sold because of the...

**The need to feel important**

**The desire for better health**

**The yearning for recognition**

**The pride of accomplishment**

**The longing for love**

**The desire for romance/ romantic fulfillment**

**The urge to look attractive/ feel beautiful/ appear more desirable**

**The lust for power**

**The yearning for independence**

**The craving for financial stability**

**The need to feel secure/ salvation**

**The hunger for self esteem/ self-regard**

**The hunger for peer or community recognition**

**The fear of loss**

**The fear of shame**

**The fear of the unknown**

We'll refer to this list again a little later. Which emotional drivers could be behind your prospects desire to buy? Once you realize the emotional foundation below the surface, you'll know what to appeal to in your ad titles and descriptions.

## Facilitate Buying

eBay has gone a long way towards helping sellers in their endeavors, by making it easier for buyers. They've automated the entire process and provided an easy way for buyers to pay instantly through Paypal. Searching for items is easy using the Keyword Search Tool and prospective buyers can click a link to send any questions they might have to the seller, well in advance of the auction's close.

But as simplified as the system is, it can't run your business for you. You still need to be on the ball, watching your listings, addressing any issues, following up on payments and carefully packaging and shipping each item as payment is received.

Everyone buys for their own reasons. What makes one person bid on an item might not even factor into the equation for the next. It's for this reason that it's usually best to uncover every key detail about the item and bring it front and center.

Supply all the answers… every conceivable detail, solution, or response to possible objections. Leave no stone unturned. By doing so, you're eliminating all possible reasons not to do business with you and thereby opening the doors of your eBay showroom to larger and larger crowds.

It's also vitally important to maintain a Feedback Rating as close to 100% positive as you possibly can. This isn't too difficult to do, as long as you accurately represent your items and deliver stellar customer service. This involves answering questions, packaging items and shipping them out in a prompt, professional manner day in and day out.

Let people buy on their own terms. Paypal is a terrific tool, but it's not the favorite of all eBayers. If you only accept Paypal in your auctions, you will automatically turn away those who prefer to pay by other methods. Most do favor Paypal, but I've also received many payments (even recently) by Money Order, Check and even Cash in several different currencies.

Occasionally I'll spot a Seller who has included a message such as "Absolutely No Paypal Accepted". One can only wonder why. But if some Sellers aren't accepting it, you can bet there are plenty of buyers who prefer other methods too. If you've got your own merchant account, you can always use that to process your eBay sales, as long as it complies with the terms of the agreement between you and your service provider, or bank.

Bottom line is you want to make it as inviting and risk-free as possible for everyone who's even remotely interested in your item to go ahead and place their bids.

Break down every barrier to this crucial step. Don't give them any reason to bypass you only to spend their money elsewhere. You want maximum attention, interest, and action – that's the only way to max-out your returns.

Part of it is simply being in the right place at the right time. Before creating your listing, do a keyword search to see where the action is for other related items, and list yours there. It's always better to locate on a busy street corner than in some remote suburb that's just being developed. You want more people to find you, so you need to be where the crowds are.

It's also crucial that you choose keywords that will draw more traffic from searches. Get as many of these into your title as possible as most eBayers only search this way, since that's the default setting used for searching.

Eliminate as many hoops, speed-bumps, and hurdles as possible that can interrupt an otherwise pleasurable buying experience. The more relevant and important details you can provide, the fewer the reasons not to continue on the path to bidding and ultimately winning a great item.

Paint a glorious picture of the benefits and advantages that can be had by the winning bidder and let everybody in on it. Spread these positive vibrations and you'll widen your net. Once others can see themselves in possession of your item, enjoying the benefits themselves, they'll be much more inclined to take the necessary action. Never assume they'll take this imaginary trip without your prompting. It just doesn't happen that way for most.

Add any logical reasoning to the mix, and you give them that extra justification for following through. One way to accomplish this is to start the bidding low, and then stress the fact that there's "No Reserve" price in place and therefore, they should bid now. Doing so gets them in the game, where they stand a chance of winning simply by bidding at any level

## Get To Know Your Potential Customers

Find the market first. That in a nutshell is one of the most important keys to marketing success in any area. Before listing even a single item, you'd be well-advised to find out if there's a market for it and where you can find that market on eBay. And before you buy any inventory for your eBay business, you need to know that you can resell it at a profit.

It just makes sense from a business point of view to conduct some basic market research before spending a dollar. This may be sound, logical advice. It's also a fundamental principle that I've violated on more that one occasion.

See, the problem arises when you assume that there's a huge market for an item you've just spotted. So you go ahead and buy it. It only hits home afterwards when you find several dozen of the exact same thing on eBay, selling for peanuts. Knowing the market and what large numbers of people want in advance can save you from the mental anguish of stocking up on inventory that's difficult to barely break even on.

Your best bet is to specialize in one or more specific areas of interest. Get a feel for the kinds of things these buyers want and are willing to freely spend on.

Put yourself in your buyer's shoes and imagine what she might be thinking… feeling… and hoping for in her life. What most people want is the internal RESULT they get from the transaction, rather than the item itself. It's the benefits – the payoff – the buyer ultimately wants. They think they're buying a product, but what they're actually paying for is the feeling.

Your job as seller is to identify these major "wants" of the individual niche market and to cater to those wants specifically. Identify key features that help deliver the benefits people desire and provide proof in the form of customer testimonials. Spot a hungry market and discover what it is that particular market really wants. They want a trimmed-down figure.... or that gleaming finish on the car. Once you've identified the end result they want -- all you have to do is deliver it.

If you want a surefire path to success on eBay, here it is: discover what it is that people want… and provide exactly that, over and over again.

Make yourself known as a premier seller of choice within the market niche and you're well on your way. Once you've tapped into a source of supply for in-demand products and you've got a bit of a track record of outstanding customer service, crowds of hungry buyers will be driven to your eBay doorstep. All you need to do is create good photos, prepare a powerful title, and then write a brief description. You want to grab attention, highlight your item's major advantages, and instigate action in the form of instant buys or bids.

## Learn From Your Competitors

Few sellers realize that not only is eBay an excellent source of sales, it's also a valuable resource for conducting research. You get to see firsthand what sells and what doesn't. You can also easily expose the various strategies applied and how they may have had an impact on the individual results of an auction.

Punch in various keywords that apply to your product and category and peruse the various items listed. Take note of any sellers who offer the same items you do, as well as those who feature multiple items in your niche category. These are the guys you want to pay particular attention to. Why? Because chances are, they've already reached a level of success. It's also a good idea to do an Advanced Search and see how their listings have performed recently.

Notice the categories used by other sellers to market their items. One category might appear obvious to you, yet another may prove more profitable. Deciding which categories to list in begins with an analysis of where your competition advertises.

Build a list of specific keywords used by these and other competitors. This is crucial. But it's the keywords used in their titles that are of the greatest significance. The reason for this is that typically eBay searches only involve the words used in listing titles, and not descriptions. This makes for more efficient searching and leaner lists of relevant auctions. eBayers are forced to go the extra mile through advanced searching to also include descriptions in their search for related keywords. This extra step, plus the fact that many users are unaware of it means the keywords in your body copy are only of secondary value.

Study the descriptions used by others as though you were a detective looking for vital clues. What main appeals are used? Has the seller stressed benefits? Is there a strong offer? Is it easily readable and well-presented? Is there a guarantee or return policy used? Does the overall listing look appealing to first-time buyers? Does this look like a seller you'd do business with? Are there obvious attributes about the seller's business or level of service that are made apparent? And most importantly, has the seller provided enough reasons for buying?

As you learn more about what works and what doesn't in terms of sales copy, you'll gain valuable insights as to how to make your eBay listings even more effective.

Pay attention to any of the optional eBay options such as Bold or Featured Listings used by other successful sellers. Does it work for them by attracting more bids? If so, it's probably worth trying with your own listings.

## Simple Keys To Successful eBay Selling

Make every listing a test listing. Not only should you set out to sell the item in each listing, you should also try to learn something from the experience. Testing enables you to learn based on actual experience rather than mere theory.

Direct response marketers know the value of testing and it's something that serious sellers could utilize just as effectively. Testing is the only way to know for sure which strategy, headline, title, offer, or ad description works best in a given market. Without putting your decisions to the test in the marketplace, you're really only guessing. Your guess may be accurate, or it may be way off. Only testing different options will give you evidence as to the best ways to proceed.

The key to effective testing is to test only one element each time. If you make more than one modification to your listing, you cannot be sure which change was responsible for producing an alternate result. But make just one change, for example, one of the keywords in your title, and you could quickly find out which version draws more viewers and bids.

It's imperative that you remain flexible in your approach to your listings. If any kind of change produces an improved result, be adaptable enough to go with the change. If it doesn't make a noticeable improvement, move on and test something else. But even the exact same titles and descriptions can produce dramatically different results from one week to the next. Such is the nature of eBay.

Focus your ads on exactly what it is that buyers want. Deliver the item's features and benefits in all your descriptions and target your message to the group of people likely to be most interested.

Lay out all the big juicy benefits that can only belong to the winner. Lots of people dislike being 'sold'… yet they love to buy when their desire has been kindled. Some rush to buy at the slightest bit of interest, while others need much more information and detail before they'll cross that emotional threshold. If you fail to provide an important tidbit of information, you risk losing a percentage of potential buyers, resulting in fewer bids and lower prices.

If they'll gladly pay for high-end sportswear, it makes no sense to build a business on cheap knock-offs. By the way, most people have little respect for cheap products and prefer items that are well-made and longer lasting.

Quality merchandise sells in good times and bad. There will always be a market for topnotch items and selling only those, means you can feel good about what you're doing. Buyers will feel good about their purchases too. Most will gladly pay a premium for higher quality products because they're getting much more in use value or ownership value than it costs in monetary value.

You can save yourself loads of heartache by steering clear of damaged goods. Unless you own an electronics repair shop, it doesn't generally pay to get into the market of selling broken down electronics, even when you're clear about this in your descriptions.

Some buyers will jump in and bid, confident in their ability to repair the item and make it good as new again. But trouble brews when they discover that the problem is actually something else they can't easily (or cheaply) fix and they want to return the item for a full refund. This end result doesn't benefit anyone, least of all the seller. Avoid junky, defective items and learn to package your items with great care. Do that and you'll eliminate 99% of potential problems before they a have a chance to take hold.

## Do It Differently

Act in the same manner with essentially the same photographs, titles and descriptions as your competitors and the best you can hope for is the same kind of results. Realistically however, you'll fare even worse if you take the identical path as another seller who's already entrenched in a particular market niche on eBay.

You need to differentiate yourself at every turn. Selling the same merchandise as others isn't necessarily a bad thing. With red-hot items, there's room for multiple sellers to earn healthy profits. Even in markets without the same level of demand, you can still give yourself a decided advantage over others by creating unique offers that feature the same item as others are selling. The trick here is to offer or package more into the deal, making your proposal stand out from the rest.

If you're marketing the same musical instruments, you can prepare a simple report that features multiple links for free music instruction... or other relevant and helpful sites and include it as a free gift. Now you're not just selling the same thing as the next guy. You've packaged it differently and added *extra* value. In a head-to-head competition for business, who do you think has the advantage?

Find a unique approach and pack more punch into your offer. Don't simply enter the arena as another option to the eBay marketplace. An experienced seller will most certainly have the upper hand in this situation, simply due to the fact that he's been around for a while and established a reputation in that niche. Set yourself apart from the outset and you'll likely draw enough attention to your listings to net a tidy profit.

## Use Stories

Everyone loves a good story. Most of us hunger for them and have since our earliest years. Author Elie Wiesel wrote *"There is something in the story which is almost eternal. God created man because he loves stories"*. The late author, Joseph Campbell said *"we all hunger for stories."* Writing teacher, Robert McKee claims *"Storytelling is the most powerful way to put ideas into the world today."* And the late poet, Muriel Rukeyser stated *"The universe is made of stories, not atoms."*

For the eBay seller, the most important thing to remember is that stories sell. I'm not talking about fake, over-hyped "tales" that are pure exaggeration. I'm talking about true stories that add realism as they engage and involve prospects.

Stories help build a connection between buyer and seller. Stories help clarify the value or use of something through verbal illustrations and examples. Stories smooth the path by making something more familiar when previously it was unknown to another. And stories make your benefits more believable by putting them in a context that can be better understood and appreciated.

Who can argue with a story? Truth is… no one can. They might not willingly accept your selling points, but they can't very well reject the story because they have no basis from which to do so.

It's a story – nothing more, nothing less – and as such, it bypasses critical analysis. It's the most direct route to your prospective buyer's subconscious mind. Your story is accepted as true by association. So too are your selling points. A good story stirs up feelings much more effectively than factual statements about your item.

When used in your eBay listings, stories can be just as powerful as in one-on-one communication. Stories help to sell. They can add color, vibrancy and action to even the most basic or standard item. Share a small story about your item and you'll overcome doubt and resistance. A particularly effective story element can add value to your item.

If your item has an interesting history, by all means, share it. People love stories. It adds relevance and value, while pulling prospects in and endearing them to you.

When buyers stumble across your auction, yours is just one of many other listings. Competition for the viewer's time and attention is unlimited on eBay and at any given time you're only a split second away from losing what could be a high-price bidder. Without a good story accompanying your item, price becomes the primary concern by default. A good story can warm up a cold audience fast and make you a seller worth doing business with.

While looking for a book recently, I came across a number of sellers offering Clinton's book, "My Life". Most were getting a few dollars for used copies, while new copies were selling at close to retail.

Other sellers had copies that were personally autographed by the former President. Most of those copies were selling for considerably more money – one to two hundred dollars or more.

But one seller I noticed got more than $500 for his autographed copy. What made the difference? He told a better story and he did it with both words and pictures. He had various snapshots of the long line-up at a popular bookstore in New York City. He shared what it took to actually be there and to get an autograph from the former President, face-to-face. The result was that his "story" built credibility. I'm sure no one even questioned whether the signature was authentic because of the shared details. And the extra money it brought in was pure profit. Tell a better story and you'll reap a bigger reward.

A story helps bring your product to life. You can share some of its' history… or at least your knowledge of the industry at large. Imagine that you're selling a cup and saucer set. If you've had it for years, you might have some "inside" information you could share. If not, you could do some research on the piece and find out where it was made, when and what methods were used. Doing so adds charm, interest and value to the item and it makes you a more interesting and knowledgeable seller -- and that's never a bad thing.

What kind of information can help you build a story? Consider something you've done with the item… somewhere you've been… something it's helped you accomplish.

How did you come upon the item? What impact did it have on you? What gave it value in your eyes? Is there a big event that you can connect to the item? Is there something unusual or rare about this piece?

You can in fact build an interesting story around almost any item if you look deep enough. It's easy to gloss this over and go onto your next listing. But before you do, consider how much money you might be leaving behind. I've made this mistake myself when I sold a knapsack that accompanied me on my European adventure, fresh out of school. This particular knapsack had been to several different countries in Europe and I had the photographs to prove it. Had I shared some of my personal experiences as a naive kid in a foreign country with nothing but the sack on my back, I might have earned more from the sale.

See, stories give meaning to objects or items. That 1851 glass vase isn't just another vase when you reveal important details about the shop, and town it was made in. By adding facts, you add richness, value and meaning. A simple story adds enlightenment, entertainment and emotion.

Arrange the details you uncover more dynamically and the emotional effect is even greater. Remember, it's emotions that drive human behavior. So the more emotional effect you inject -- the more potential the selling price.

You can use stories with practically any item you list. Your Title and Gallery Image inspired prospects to click on your listing. They're interested to some degree or they wouldn't have bothered to click. But a lack of familiarity with any item translates into a lack of action. Enter your story.

Here's where you can shift your prospect's focus from hesitation due to the unknown, to one where they get wrapped up in the story and emotionally involved with the product. With the aid of your story, the value of your item becomes much clearer.

Tell your prospects what it is that makes your item unique. That's all it takes to create a story. If it has a rich history, share it with feeling and you'll build an emotional connection.

If your item helps solve a problem, reveal how challenging it was to deal with the burden before you (or another customer) discovered the solution… and how much easier it is now.

Build a short story that proves your claims and provides evidence that it does what you say it does. Anticipate potential objections and knock the legs out from under them with a simple story of how someone, somewhere did it.

Stories are a proven way to inject additional advantages in a meaningful way. You had a problem and bought what you thought was a solution. But what you received didn't just solve the original problem, it also solved others unexpectedly. Now that's a powerful way to supply evidence, added value, and uniqueness to your listings. It's something your prospects rarely get from other merchants.

Simply describe the end result of having the product or item. Paint a vibrant picture your prospects can easily relate to. Allow them to mentally take ownership of the new results and you've made an important connection. Stories can be an important element of your selling message. I encourage you to use a story whenever you can and improve your overall eBay sales results.

# Chapter Six: Getting Started

Preparation Meets Opportunity
3 Key Elements
How To Find The Largest Pool of Prospective Buyers
How To Discover Valuable Information About Your Item
What Every Potential Buyer Wants To Know About You
Establishing Unique Advantages

The purpose of this chapter is to help you speed up the process of creating listings – while at the same time, writing ads that sell. We'll explore quick-start methods to finding your market and creating short, easy to write ads that work like magic.

Is it possible to create a powerful listing in just 5 minutes or less? Yes it is. Read on and you'll discover several approaches you can adopt as your own to crank out more effective ads in a fraction of the time.

## Preparation Meets Opportunity

eBay affords you and me an opportunity like no other. When I started researching this topic, eBay had 140 million registered users worldwide and it's growing by 80,000 new names each and every day. That's one gigantic marketplace and it's available to every seller. What's more, it's dirt cheap for a seller to create an ad and post it on eBay. You get worldwide marketing exposure instantly for pennies. Never has the independent entrepreneur yielded such marketing clout on a global basis before. So it's worthwhile to learn how to get the most from your listings.

eBay has and continues to revolutionize buying and selling for millions of people. But you can only take advantage of this unprecedented opportunity to the maximum when you do your homework. Sure, anybody could sell almost any item at any time.

You might even get lucky and make thousands of dollars in profit from a single item and transaction. I hope that happens for you. I've experienced this kind of result on a few occasions myself.

But serious sellers know they need to create new listings every day. As your listings expire, you're left with fewer items to showcase, and therefore less potential profit. So you need to continually be bringing in additional items and making these available to your customers on eBay.

Creating lots of listings is one key to improving your revenue because the more items you have, the more eyeballs you'll attract to your eBay business. Posting items on eBay is the most effective and productive use of your time as a seller. The more stuff you have available to buyers, the higher your earning potential. That's easy for anyone to understand. But placing more items on display doesn't necessarily mean bigger profits. All it does is increase your exposure.

You're better off to assess your profit potential before you list each individual item. Doing so could save you hours of time each month and no small amount of frustration.

If your item is available in countless other places online or offline for $1.95 -- it's not worth even a few minutes of your time to create that listing. Conversely, if your item stands to bring in a few hundred dollars or more in profit, it's probably worth spending some time to craft a powerful ad and thereby do your part to maximize your earnings.

It's the value or the potential profit that determines how much time and attention you should devote to each product listing. If all you want is a sale to gain some experience and hopefully build up your Feedback score, then by all means, feel free to create whatever listings you want and start the bidding as low as possible. But if you're looking for a long-term solution, learn to quickly assess each item as it comes to you. If you can make a quick and impressive profit, it's probably worth using the strategies in this book to create a fast listing that will help you sell it and earn maximum profit. You've got to decide on the items that are worthy of your investment in time and try to locate more of those with a high payoff potential.

Make the best use of your listing time. For example... it's more productive to create your listings in numbers. I like to shoot for ten at a time. Once I've got ten items I think will sell at an attractive enough profit, I shift into sales mode and start writing my listings.

One of the most important tips I can give you is to begin with a clear, calm state of mind. If you're uptight or overly stressed out about anything, you may have a tendency to just post listings for the sake of getting more "stuff" up on eBay. Don't do it. Go for a brisk walk instead. Stretch your muscles. Do a five-minute meditation. Breathe deeply over and over again, taking in as much oxygen as you can, holding it, and then exhaling completely. Whatever works for you to calm you down and revitalize your energy is the remedy I suggest you use. With a clear head and an energized spirit, you're ready to dive right in and start the multiple listings process.

Before you begin, there's just one more thing I'm going to suggest. Clear off the desk or table you're using entirely. Return all file folders to their respective drawers. Place all pens and pencils in holders. Remove all clutter so you're not distracted in any way once you get started with your 10 (or whatever number works for you) listings. Now with a clear surface and a clear mind, you're ready to create some killer ads that could bring you lots of cash fast.

## 3 Key Elements

There are just 3 key elements to the sales cycle on eBay. Those 3 elements are:

### 1. The Product or Item...

**2. The Marketplace (Your Prospects and Customers)...** and...

**3. The Seller (You).**

In other words, the seller has a product and wants to sell it to someone else. So there's a seller, and item to sell, and the prospective buyer. It's basic stuff that should be easy to understand. But it's often overlooked. As a result, money (and lots of it) is left on the table by sellers who simply didn't pay attention to each of the three components of every transaction.

What kind of products are people interested in? Buyers tend to spend money for a variety of reasons and every reason has a strong emotional component. Nobody buys things they don't want. But they often buy things they don't need. How many "things" do we really need anyway? So first and foremost, if you want to succeed as a seller, you have to sell the kinds of things that people want.

Judging by some of the results I've seen on eBay, you have to wonder just what people were thinking to spend the kind of money to acquire certain things. But we're all different and we respond in unique ways. If you happen to luck out with a bizarre item that people spend an outrageous amount of money to acquire for you – good for you. Just don't bank your business on that sort of thing happening frequently.

Instead, focus on providing solid items that lots of people want. Quality never goes out of style. When you sell brand name merchandise with a solid reputation, you're offering something that retains a certain amount of value. Everyone wants good value for their money.

People buy value when they exchange their cash for your goods. The item must possess more in *use value* than they'll pay in *cash value*. It may be an item like a lawnmower that they use themselves. Perhaps it's a book they hope to read someday, or a collectible to hold onto for years as an investment. Maybe it's something they buy to simply resell themselves. Whatever the desire at the time, the "use value" must exceed the cost in cash, or no buy takes place.

What does your marketplace want to buy? Well, that's exactly the kinds of items you need to supply. Choose a couple of specific categories and roll up your sleeves. Identify which items attract the most attention and higher bids. Keep an ongoing list of the things each specific pool of buyers is anxious to acquire. As you set out to acquire inventory to sell, refer to your list often.

You might never find the items that are highest in demand. After all, they're rare and hard to find and it's the old 'supply and demand' axiom that comes into play here. Nevertheless, know what your market will pay the most for and keep your eyes open for these items.

You can do very well on eBay selling other items at a profit. But it means knowing what items specific markets want and how much they'll generally pay for those items. Armed with this information, you know exactly what to seek out at wholesale and how much you can afford to pay to still turn a healthy profit.

Success on eBay is largely about offering what it is that people already want, rather than trying to sell whatever it is you happen to have on hand.

Sellers make up the third and final element of the eBay experience. And you're not just selling products, you're selling yourself.

eBayers love to buy. But the fact is, almost everyone has been ripped off before at some point in their lives. It might have been years or decades earlier, but the painful experienced was burned deep into the memory bank. Somewhere along the line, your potential customer was cheated. On at least one other occasion, they got much less than they bargained for. The cumulative result of this raw deal is that they're deathly afraid of it happening again.

Your job as a merchant is to calm those fears and create a comfortable scenario where fear is no longer a factor. You want people to feel safe, secure and 100% confident in bidding on your item -- knowing that if they win, they'll promptly get from you exactly what they expect.

Buyers are most eager to do business with sellers who are honest and reliable. They appreciate sellers who offer full disclosure in each listing, revealing the less attractive elements in addition to the positive attributes that more accurately reflect the item listed.

Feedback is invaluable in presenting yourself as a seller worthy of a buyer's business. The closer you can get to 100% Positive Feedback, the more appealing it is to go ahead and take a chance on you. The perception of the buyer is this: the closer to 100% your Feedback Rating is, the lower the risk in dealing with you, provided of course, you have some kind of track record.

If you're brand new to eBay, it's very difficult to sell without at least 10 positive feedbacks. The more you've been around and the more favorable the experience of other eBayers, the more likely it is others feel confident to proceed.

Incidentally, your Feedback score works the same whether you're a buyer or seller. So you can get started by going out and buying a bunch of inexpensive items and collecting positive feedback.

If you've got a track record of performance and it looks impressive, you've eliminated a potential roadblock to a profitable sale.

Quality responses should be a primary goal. While there's no way to control the actual comments you receive, you can certainly do your part to create a positive experience. As a buyer, the best thing you can do is to pay immediately at the close of the transaction and the fastest method to do so is Paypal.

As a seller, it's important to deliver on every promise and to provide exceptional customer service. This means answering all inquiries promptly and professionally… carefully packaging each item… and shipping in the most expedient way possible.

Keep it simple. Nobody likes to read and decipher half a page of shipping options before deciding to bid. They want straightforward answers, clearly listed total costs, and super-smooth transactions. The more you deliver this, the more prospective buyers will be drawn to bid on your items.


## How To Find The Largest Pool of Prospective Buyers

Before considering each listing, take the time to peruse the eBay directory and build a list of all possible categories each product could conceivably be listed in. For example, you could find a book or CD on golf techniques in...

1) Sporting Goods>Golf>Training Aids>Other Training Aids
2) Books>Audio books
3) Sporting Goods>Golf>Other

But what you really want to know before you list your instructional golf program is which of those categories is likely the most profitable location to present your listing. You can take a guess, if you like. Maybe you'll get it right and maybe you won't. You can enter your topic on eBay in this field -- SELL: Select a Category

A more effective approach is to go back and see where others have had the most success recently and follow their lead. eBay makes this easy to do. Simply go to Advanced Search and enter your keyword of choice. You can find a link to advanced search just below the Search field at the top right corner of most eBay pages.

In this case, you might enter something like "golf instruction". As results are returned to you, take a look at the table on the left side of the page. It's the one with the yellow background. I just did this as I'm writing these words and I found products listed in several categories including Sporting Goods, DVD's and Movies, Books, Sports Memorabilia, Cards and Fan Shop – even Music and Video Games. Clearly most were listed under Sporting Goods with 57 listings, followed by DVD's and Movies with 23, and Books with 7 listings. Sports Memorabilia, Cards and Fan Shop had 3, while the Music and Video categories had 2 each.

Based on these numbers, if I had to choose one location for my listing, it looks like Sporting Goods would make the best choice. But there's another result to investigate before making that call.

Click the Back button in your browser and return to the Advanced Search window. As we re-enter "Golf Instruction" in the Search Field, we also click the "Completed Listings Only" box. Next, scroll down to the bottom of the page. In the "Sort by" field, choose "Price: Highest First" and then hit the Search button below.

Now look at the categories that housed those listings which attracted the highest bids while using the search term "Golf Instruction". Look at the table to the left and see that the same general categories were returned. Now it's time to delve a little deeper.

Scroll through the results looking for "selling prices" highlighted in green. This indicates items that actually sold. Click on each "sold" listing and then look at the top of the page to identify the specific category the listing appeared in. You'll find and expanded category like this…

Sporting Goods > Golf > Books, Videos > Videos

or…

DVD's and Movies > DVD

Check out several such listings and pay particular attention to categories selected by those sellers to feature their Golf Instruction items. There's no hard and fast rule as to which one to choose. But the results should give you a good indication of what will work best for you, based on what worked for other sellers recently (within the past 30 days).

There are only two ways buyers can find your listings on eBay:

>    **1. Keyword Searching...** and
>    **2. Category Searching.**

Most people have limited free time these days. So they want to make the most of their time on eBay. That's why the lion's share of eBayers seek the items they want by entering a relative keyword or phrase in the Search box.

Some still scroll through multiple pages of listings in their favorite category. But shopping this way is becoming increasingly time-consuming as eBay continues to grow larger by the day. So keyword searching will likely continue to grow in popularity and usage – and that's something you should pay attention to maximize your results.

If everyone only used keywords, individual categories would play a less important role. But your intention should always be to attract as many people as possible to your ads to give you the largest pool of interested buyers. Larger crowds usually mean more bids and higher selling prices.

Be sure to consider all relevant possibilities in terms of categories. Think about the most logical location first. Ultimately, your decision boils down to locating your little ad where the maximum number of prospective buyers can find you quickly and easily on eBay.

## How To Discover Valuable Information About Your Item

Okay, so you've found a category or two that holds potential for your item. But what's going to make anyone interested in your item when there are literally hundreds of thousands of other choices and perhaps even more interesting items?

First of all, a change in perspective is in order. It doesn't really matter what you're selling. There's a good chance someone else will want it and they'll gladly give up some of their cash to get it.

Now, it's important to focus on high-demand products whenever possible. But never assume for a moment that the individual item you'd love to get rid of isn't of great interest and value to others. Keep an open mind. Just because that old circular saw left in the attic for 27 years because you had no use for it, doesn't mean that someone else wouldn't gladly pay you handsomely for it. There's value in everything... *but it's up to you to uncover it.*

Place the item before you. Jot down any words, thoughts, or feelings that come to mind. For example, that old saw that sat untouched all those years, might evoke the following notes...

> Remarkably good condition for its age
> Brand name
> Hardened Steel Blade
> Elaborate Wooden Handle with Handgrip
> Removable Blade
> Used for?
> Looks almost new
> Made in the USA

As words get scribbled onto the page, you begin to notice the inherent value of the item before you. What was once just a dusty old saw is now something that serious tool collectors might be interested in.

Ask yourself questions about the item. Where did it come from? Who owned it before? Where was it made? How did you acquire it? What is it used for? Is it available today through traditional (retail) channels? What condition is it in? Are there other such models available? What is the actual size and weight? What comes with it?

The above questions are simply idea starters. Not all apply to every item. You likely may even have better questions of your own. Whatever the case may be, give it some thought for a minute or two and record your answers as they appear. The trick is to gather as much raw data as you can and then fill in the nitty-gritty details later.

Take whatever brief information you have on the item and do a search online. Simply go to Google or another search engine and enter a few details about your item.

I did this recently with that old saw and found some surprising results. What I discovered was that it wasn't just another saw, as it was no longer being manufactured. I probably would have happily accepted $20 before. Now I figured I could possibly get three times as much. When I finally got around to selling it, I got a little over $100 – 5 times higher than I would have accepted earlier.

Had I jumped the gun and listed it as just another saw carpenter's use, chances are I would have received only ho-hum results.

Discover what it is about each item that gives it value. What makes it interesting… unique… useful… or worth more than other such items?

If there's anything different about it, you've got to find out what that difference is. Collectible postage stamps that feature printing errors like reversed images are rare. But it's this kind of detail that makes one stamp worth thousands more than another.

Once you've gathered some details about the item or product, consider what it is the buyer actually gets. So far, all your data is strictly about the item itself. It's all FEATURES. But what buyers are most interested in is what the item (and its features) gives them.

It's the emotional payoff that makes people want to buy. You've heard me say that before. But it's so important, that it bears repeating. In other words – it's the perceived benefits they buy. Yes, features are important on eBay. Prospective buyers want to know the specifics about a product. But what triggers an avalanche of bids and higher and higher prices is the imagined emotional reward of ownership.

There's one more thing to consider here. What is it about your item that makes it a great buy or a genuine bargain? Since most folks turn to eBay to find great deals, this is a key issue. You need to be cognizant of the presence of this bargain-hunter mindset that prevails in most categories.

The easiest (although it's also the most gutsy) thing to do is to offer a high value item at an exceptionally low starting bid, with no reserve. These listings attract maximum eyeballs because of the stark contrast between the high perceived value of the item and the low asking price. The risk to you as a seller is that your item sells too low. But if you focus the majority of your efforts on products that are in large demand this shouldn't be too much of a concern.

## What Every Potential Buyer Wants To Know About You

Every single bidder wants to know that they can go ahead and bid with confidence. They want to feel reasonably assured that...

> 1) You've accurately represented the item and you'll ship it out in a timely and effective manner and...

2) That you're worthy of their trust and they won't get ripped off.

Present yourself as a credible person and reputable business. But all any fellow eBayer has to go on to distinguish one seller from the next is their user name, the Feedback Score tied to that name, and their own previous experience with the seller. Most user names are nothing more than disguises. Buyers don't really have much of a clue who they're dealing with when they stumble upon an interesting listing – unless they recognize he seller's name and have had past dealings with the same seller. Knowing the user's name is "imadufusru12" doesn't make anyone any more confident to proceed.

But what can make a huge difference is a seller's Feedback Rating. I find the eBay Feedback System to be both brilliant and incredibly frustrating. Brilliant because it gives every user the opportunity to share brief details and rate their overall satisfaction with the transaction and the item purchased. But it's also frustrating when you bend over backwards to serve your customers and they turn around and leave you neutral or negative feedback.

It makes me a little crazy, particularly when their beef is due to the time it takes for the post office to deliver the parcel. Once a package is turned over for delivery to the post office, there's nothing the seller can do except pray the package reaches its destination intact and in a timely manner. But when it doesn't, you better brace yourself for the fallout.

Thankfully, 99% of the time, that's exactly what happens. But once in a while, the voodoo dolls come out to play and your shipment goes astray. I've had everything from lost packages that never turn up to those that resurface inexplicably a month or two after the fact with an "undeliverable to this address" label – even though it's the exact address provided by the buyer. As far as the buyer is concerned, he's unhappy because of the delay and feels justified in leaving you negative feedback – even though you did your part to the best of your ability. Such is the life of an eBay seller.

See… the buyer doesn't know you. Chances are it's his first transaction with you. Let's suppose he goes ahead and bids… and actually wins your item. At this point, your buyer is ecstatic and filled with anticipation. But as each day passes with no item in sight, that happy anticipation turns into an agonizing wait.

The winning bidder hopes that you shipped the item straight away and that you got the address right. But he has no personal experience in dealing with you. All he has to go on is the feedback previous buyers or sellers have left. If all your feedback indicates that you're an upfront and honest seller, the buyer probably feels some reassurance. In fact, he probably wouldn't have even bid unless there was an adequate level of comfort and security.

Buyers on eBay are like buyers anywhere else. They want to feel as though the seller values them and that if there's ever a problem (such as a lost shipment) that they will be taken care of -- either by receiving a replacement item, or a full and immediate refund. Buyers want to feel safe and secure and assured that they'll get exactly what you promised in your listing, without any excuses.

## Establishing Unique Advantages

Go deep. That's the key to unearthing ideas and concepts that can really add perceived value to your item in the eyes of the marketplace. Look beyond the obvious stuff you see on the surface. Most sellers use very little detail when describing their items and often the details shared aren't the most important ones.

One of the first things to look for is product reviews. Many such reviews exist online. One huge site with lots of reviews is amazon.com.

Amazon started as an online bookseller but they've since branched out to include many different types of consumer products. Simply visit the site and type in the name of your item. If you can't find a review there, search the web for one. Chances are pretty good that if it's a somewhat recent product, you can find a review of it online. The more reviews you can find, the better. This gives you more material to draw from.

Look for small tidbits of information that could be the key to a potential buyer. If a well-known authority in the field said something positive and unique about your item, consider using their exact words as an endorsement. If a major home-renovation magazine field-tested the efficiency of your solar heating system and they reported favorable results, be sure to mention this in your description.

What you're looking for is the kind of detail prospects are wondering about. By addressing such in your listing, you're answering their questions and objections – head on. If the information comes from a credible source (a publication, author, or area expert) it helps prove your claims. Most people tend to believe the words of an outside source over the seller's own words simply because they assume a seller will tell them whatever they want to hear, in order to close the deal.

Take a look at what other sellers use to sell the same item. Again, use eBay's Advanced Search function to see if the same item sold in the past 30 days and if it did, what other sellers wrote in their descriptions to make the sale. This is especially valuable when you see multiple sales and a wide variation in prices. You'll find that the best advertising usually fetches the highest prices.

Transform every physical characteristic of the item into something of greater emotional value to the prospect. Turn features into benefits by taking out a blank sheet of paper and drawing a line down the middle of the page. At the top of the page, write "Features" on the left side and "Benefits" on the right. Now take a few brief moments to list the plain facts about your chosen item.

For example, I've placed a small picture frame on the desk in front of me. I'm going to jot down a few simple features that come to mind.

**Black lacquer finish**
**Metal**
**4 x 6**
**Sliding mechanism**
**2-way stand**
**Built-in hook holder**
**Plastic backing**
**No pins**
**Glass front**

Creating this list took all of about 30 seconds. I simply examined the item and then typed in words that described some individual aspect of the picture frame. Now let's take this list and make it mean something more to a prospective buyer.

| <u>Item Feature</u> | <u>Corresponding Benefit to Buyer</u> |
|---|---|
| *Black lacquer finish* | This means you get a beautiful, stylish, and durable finish that looks great with any décor. |
| *Metal* | This rugged frame is made from the strongest picture frame material possible -- so it will last for years and years. |
| *4 inches x 6* | Compact size means it's perfect for standard prints. |
| *Sliding mechanism* | It's quick and easy to change the photo at any time. Just slide the photo in and lock it in place – no |

muss, no fuss. No tools required. It's so easy, anyone could do this.

*2-way stand*

Displays perfectly -- horizontally or vertically -- on any flat surface which allows you to present any 4x6 image beautifully.

*Built-in hook holder*

This feature gives you struggle-free, perfect wall-mounting in just seconds. No flexible hooks to worry about. Just find a hook and you're done – it's that easy.

*Plastic backing*

Forget unsightly cardboard that doesn't last. This backing is solid, durable plastic that's resistant to spills. It's a rugged frame, designed to last for decades.

*No pins*

Ever struggle to get it just right when using pins or glaziers points to hold the picture, matting and glass all together? Forget about it! With this system, it's the easiest thing in the world to install or change your photographs.

*Glass front*

If you want your picture to look great for decades, glass is the only way to go. It's much more scratch-resistant than even the most advanced plastic. The perfectly polished glass front completes this beautiful and luxurious shiny black picture frame.

Sure, this more detailed look took considerably longer -- about 7 minutes in total. But do you see the value in this exercise?

Now we have some usable details that could help this picture frame sell on eBay. If you were selling this exact item, you might have chosen different benefits based to focus on.

Was this 7-minute exercise necessary? No. You might very well be able to sell this same frame without bothering with the details. But if you don't add some emotional value to the mix, there'll be less incentive to buy and that can only mean less money for you.

Uncover every shred of proof you can find to back your claims. I once sold a book autographed by the late Og Mandino. At first I simply listed the item and mentioned that it was indeed autographed in blue pen. One interested buyer requested an image of the autograph itself, which I was happy to provide. But I should have included this image from the get go as it was proof to the serious prospect that the book had indeed been signed by the author.

Another great autograph strategy is to include a few photographs of the event in which the autograph was obtained. Think of collectible trading card shows… book signings… consumer and trade shows... or other public events. Take snapshots while you're there and include these in your listings. It adds personality and credibility, which ultimately means more money in your pocket. That's exactly how that seller mentioned earlier got top dollar for the Clinton book.

To maximize profits, it's important to present your item in an appealing way. Highlight the item and make it the star of the show. Consider it from every angle and decipher every benefit. If there are any extras you can include, such as a carrying case for your camera, an original owners manual, or even the box an item came in originally – be sure to do so. Anything related to the item can help increase its value.

## Chapter Seven: The Basic, Time-Tested Selling Formula That Works Everywhere

A Proven Formula
Basic Selling Ideas
Use Short Paragraphs, Sentences, Words and Segments
Take The Long Term View

### A Proven Formula

There's one foundational selling formula that's been around for years. It's called AIDA… and it means…

> **A -- Attention**
> **I -- Interest**
> **D -- Desire**
> **A -- Action**

This simple-four-part formula has stood the test of time from it's inception in the 1940's for one simple reason – it works. When you first grab the ATTENTION of your prospect and draw them inside your message with something of great INTEREST and then you stoke their DESIRE to the point where they simply must take ACTION and buy, your ad has done its job.

Many other formulas exist, but virtually all of them have the components of AIDA within. It's a short formula that's easy to remember. And it works exceedingly well. Commit this simple, 4-step strategy to memory and use it to your advantage in your listings. As you become more proficient at it, your overall results will improve automatically, as you won't have to stop and think about what comes next.

Let's take a brief look at each element.

1.  **Attention** – Every eBay listing needs to attract an audience
    – first and foremost. You simply have to catch
    shoppers/browsers/prospects INSTANTLY as they scroll
    through a category, or their fresh new window of eBay
    Search Results.

    The initial attention-getting task is the responsibility of the
    Title, Gallery Image and Sub-Title (if used). Of these three
    elements, the TITLE is most important. Only words used in
    the Title are available in the default searches on eBay. So if
    your keyword isn't included in the main title, your listing
    won't attract maximum exposure.

    You've got to hit your target market's sweet spot – quickly
    and definitively -- with a Title that catches their attention
    and pulls them inside your listing.

    You want to get the click – that's it. Get them to click on
    your Title to check out your item in detail. The best Titles
    draw the eye and generate excitement because they connect
    with what the prospect is already thinking about. A good
    Title captivates prospects -- compelling them to click
    through and read on.

2.  **Interest** – You can't begin to build serious interest if you
    don't first have your prospect's undivided attention. Once
    you've captured attention, it's vital that you deliver a
    relevant payoff that's of great interest to your momentarily
    captive audience. So your Listing has to connect to the
    Title, which is what got them interested enough to click
    through to the details page.

    Use the first few lines of your listing to confirm what
    you've got and to intensify any interest. Clearly the best
    way to do this is to pile on the benefits. Give your
    prospects benefits of value and significance. Make it clear
    how your product is helpful, time-saving, money-saving, or

life-enhancing in some way. Tailor the benefits to the specific audience you hope to reach with each new listing.

3. **Desire** -- Keep building the level of interest. Stack one benefit on top of another and build up buyer interest to the point where they not only want the item, but simply must have it. Transform mild interest into a raging desire. Desires drive people. Desire is an emotional force that emanates from within.

   Once a prospect's interest turns into a strong desire to own your item, getting them to bid is almost a sure thing.

   Make them an offer they can't refuse. Add irresistibility by providing far more value in terms of benefits and add-ons, than you ask in price. Pile on helpful and in-demand bonus items, offer some kind of a guarantee and emphasize the limitations of your offer. If you've only got one item – stress that fact.

   Converting interest into desire is all about salesmanship. You want to make your item and your offer sound so advantageous… so easy… so affordable… and the perfect solution to a problem facing interested bidders.

4. **Action** -- This is where the rubber meets the road. You either make your mark or you miss it. Your prospect either decides that "yes, this is something I want" or it's not.

   Ideally, you want positive action NOW and on eBay this means clicking the Buy-It-Now button and following through, or placing a bid. That's the objective and that's the mindset you should adopt if you want to make your listings strong, direct-response ads that get lots of action.

End listings by asking for action. In standard auctions, I remind prospects that since there's no reserve set, any bid – even of the smallest amount – could win. So it's really in their best interest to go ahead and place a bid now. The call to action is an important final step in the process… but one that many sellers seem to miss out on entirely.

It's not enough to grab the attention of target prospects, stack multiple benefits sky-high, and generate a burning desire with a superb offer and guarantee. You should also take them by the hand and get them to Buy-It-Now or place a bid.

On more expensive items, you can make it easier to buy with multiple payment options. Fortunately, eBay makes this easy to do. It's also a good idea to provide as many different ways for buyers to pay for their purchases as possible. Paypal is a must as not only is it the number one accepted payment method on eBay, but it also allows buyers to use their credit cards. Numerous other options abound too and it's never a bad idea to accommodate the largest number of buyers possible.

Make the action phase a logical and reasonable conclusion to your benefit-laden presentation. That's the key. Crank up the emotional desire to the point where the truly interested prospect finds it difficult to walk away.

There are three kinds of actions. Best of all is the Buy-It-Now option. This one closes the deal instantly at a price set by the seller. Often Buy-It-Now users pay just as quickly, so you get your money without any delay.

Secondly, prospects can place a bid. This is another form of action that you want. It means they're not just "lookie-loos" but serious in their intent to buy.

Finally, prospects can mark your listing as one to watch. This is a good indication of the level of interest in your item, though it's no guarantee you'll see any bids. Lots of eBay sellers pay attention to what others are doing. You really have no way of knowing who it is that's watching. Even if it's serious buyers, occasionally they forget about your listing, can't get online when they were going to place a bid, or simply changed their mind and spent their money elsewhere.

So the ultimate goal is to get them to buy now. Next in order of preference is to inspire bids. If you can't get that kind of action, try for a free subscription to your notification list or ezine. Finally, you want them to mark the page in hopes they'll return before your auction ends and either buy or bid at that time.

That's it... short and sweet. It's the AIDA formula applied to selling on eBay. It's an easy formula to learn and recall at will.

AIDA can be tremendously effective on its own. You can also take its basic framework and adapt it into your own formula, method, or system. But keep these basic principles in mind whenever you set out to create a new listing.

The AIDA formula is the best known and probably the oldest advertising formula ever developed. It's time-tested and proven effective beyond any shadow of doubt. With just 4 basic elements, anyone can master it.

AIDA delivers a solid foundation for advertising that works. If you used nothing but the AIDA method, you could, with a little practice develop powerful and persuasive eBay listings that bring you more action and higher selling prices.

## Basic Selling Ideas

One of the most famous names in advertising history is Claude Hopkins. It was he who labeled direct-response advertising as "Salesmanship in print". That's certainly true about magazine ads, newspaper ads, direct mail sales letters and any kind of marketing material that attempts to influence and persuade with words.

Though we're living in the golden age of technology where virtually all we could ever want is only a click or two away, Hopkins' label is just as applicable today – online and on eBay. It's salesmanship in pixels. In other words, we sell on eBay with words read on a monitor, rather than in print.

The key concept to remember is this: as a seller, you're in the business of making sales and the best way to make more sales and make more money is to use proven techniques of salesmanship. In fact, most of what Hopkins and many other great advertising geniuses, past and present discovered can be applied to your eBay listings with tremendous effectiveness.

Let's take a look at some of these "selling ideas" and how you might apply them to your eBay listings.

Use simple, everyday language. A conversational tone that's descriptive and to the point keeps readers actively involved in your message. Confuse them with fancy words and you lose them.

Same thing happens when you try to "write" rather than simply communicate in a down to earth way. The reason is that most people were taught to write in a stilted way, rather than to write the way they'd speak over coffee. Talk to a friend about your wonderful item, rather than attempting prose. It works. And it's much easier.

You want prospects to read your entire listing, even though most won't. If you're conversational in your approach, at least you've got a fighting chance. You want them to be able to understand what you're offering and the terms... to agree with your sales points... to ultimately decide to bid or buy... and to know exactly what they need to do next, to get what they want.

Be prospect-centered rather than product-centered. Most sellers get this reversed. They tell others only about the item up for auction. But the wise seller communicates from the prospects point of view. What this means is that your description is centered on what the item can do or what it means to the lucky buyer, rather than simply what it is.

One beautiful handcrafted candle is pretty much like the next one. If the description simply zeroes in on what it is, there's not much to pull buyers in by the busload. But the seller who paints a picture of a Martha Stewart type crafting a wonderful candle that delivers a beautifully scented oasis at home anytime you'd like, has a distinct advantage with a more vivid and enticing description.

Never assume your prospects will anticipate the benefits without your help. You've got to place the image in their minds, effectively doing the creative thinking for them.

Think of it as part of the service you deliver. Include all the relevant facts. But it's important to create and perpetuate the dream.

What end result does your prospect want from the item? They're at one end of the scale right now. But what they want is at the other end. Spell it out so it's easy for prospects to see themselves within the picture. If they can see it and feel it, they're more likely to want it. Help them to want what you have to offer.

Start with a brief message that delivers gold. Your Title is of supreme importance as that's the one thing that most often gets you the click-through to your auction page. But once your page opens up, what happens next?

In our click-happy world, you've got merely a split second to make an impact and build a connection with your prospect. In fact, by the time the prospect reaches your page, she might have forgotten which title she clicked on. So it's in your best interest to reiterate the keywords of your Title straight away. It's also imperative to build significant interest in whatever it is you have to offer. That's where your headline comes in.

Begin your description with a headline that offers a big promise to the right audience. Look, your prospect may be intensely interested -- or only mildly so. But she's got her finger on the trigger and is ready to flee at a moment's notice, regardless. So you've got to deliver a big promise to keep your prospect on your page and to relax somewhat that tension in her trigger finger. Tell your prospect what she'll get if she wins the auction and do so with vivid descriptions and emotional impact.

## Use Short Paragraphs, Short Sentences, Short Words and Short Segments

In our time-pressed society, nobody likes to read long passages unless it's written by a Steven King or John Grisham and those volumes are read purely for pleasure and relaxation. Shopping on eBay is engaging and action-oriented and not a passive activity. So make it easy for people to breeze through your listings. Keep them moving. If they stumble or stall, they probably move right on past your listings.

Forget about using big words when small ones will do. Forget about using long passages in your eBay descriptions because it causes prospects to flee faster than a fly within range of a swatter.

Look at the most read publications – newspapers – and emulate their short, punchy, to-the-point style. Study the articles in USA Today or the Wall Street Journal and you'll invariably find short paragraphs – particularly at the beginning. There's a very good

131

reason for this. It keeps people reading. And that's exactly the effect you want to create.

Write short sentences that contain single thoughts. Make comprehension grade-school easy. Long sentences of multiple lines can confuse even the best of readers. Potential customers aren't viewing your page to hone their skills or to read for the heck of it – they're looking for a great deal, or to acquire something they just can't find anywhere else. Since you're the one trying to make the sale, you've got to deliver your information in a user-friendly way.

Substitute short words for long wherever the meaning is not adversely impacted. If you can't find a shorter word, than go ahead and use the next best thing. But you should always favor the short word to its longer cousin if the meaning is essentially the same. Below are a few examples of using simple words that everyone understands.

Use Short Words From The First Column As Replacements For Longer Words in The Second:

Tough ……………... Difficult
Get …………….…... Receive
Tell ………….……... Inform
Use ………….……... Utilize
Show ……………..… Indicate
Place ………………. Positioning
Now ……………….. Currently
End ……………….. Finalize, Terminate
Start ………………. Initiate
Test ……………….. Experiment
Make ……………... Manufacture
Stop ……………….. Prevent
Buy ……………….... Purchase
Giant ………………. Enormous
Box ……………...… Container

Suit ……………………. Garment
See ……………………... Discern, Observe


It's also important to deliver your information in short, bite-size segments. Don't group all your elements together into one big pile. That's the same as writing page-long paragraphs. Instead, break it up to make it pleasing to the eye and more inviting to read. This is easy to accomplish in a variety of ways.

Set your headline in a larger font size. You may also choose to make it bold or set it in a contrasting style. For example, if your text is written in Arial, you can set your headline apart in a larger size of Times New Roman.

Testimonials look inviting to read when set inside a table or text box. The key elements here are a frame around the box (similar to the attention-getting device in direct mail called a Johnson Box) and the background of the box placed in offsetting color, like pale yellow when the main message is set in white.

Bullet points are another great way to deliver powerful, emotional copy in short bursts and in a way that looks visually appealing. Each bullet point acts as a mini-headline that has the power in itself to convert the unconverted.

You want your listing to attract maximum readership from true prospects. In order to accomplish this, your page can't be too daunting to tackle. Short segments are easy to devour in one quick snippet. Each one either adds to their interest level or diminishes it. That's why it's important to deliver the precise information your audience wants. Make each segment a golden nugget and you'll achieve great results by drawing more and more prospects to your auctions.

Write the listing first and then polish it up afterwards. Proofread it to catch any spelling mistakes and then organize the information to make the biggest splash for those who step inside.

## Take The Long Term View

While it's true that anyone can sell just about any thing at any given time, it's imperative that serious sellers consider the long term implications. Making that quick sale will feed you today, but the long-term approach to consistent and repeat sales will feed you in style for life.

It may surprise you as it did me just how many customers come back again and again to check out your auctions and to buy more goods. At last check, nearly a full 50% of the Feedback I had received came from repeat buyers. It might have been the second or third time a buyer left feedback and therefore my total Feedback Score didn't change. But my "all positive feedback received" number changed significantly. What this means is that nearly half of all the people who left positive feedback had already done so and therefore, it didn't increase my rating. But the fact that so many had become repeat buyers underscores the value of creating a positive experience for customers.

Customers return because of their previous positive experiences. In other words, they feel that they got at least as much as they bargained for and overall, feel as though they came out on top. If they didn't feel that way, you can bet they wouldn't return and they could possibly leave you negative feedback as well.

If you pull out all the stops to make the sale and maximize your earnings today, just be sure that you don't sugar-coat your offer and hide its negatives. That's the kind of approach you might expect from a shady used car salesperson who fails to disclose that the car you're about to buy was involved in a serious accident and consequently sustained damages not readily apparent to the naked and inexperienced eye. Full, honest disclosure is essential to survival and growth in a competitive marketplace. Think beyond the sale.

Your first sale to any customer-- on eBay or in any other arena – is usually the hardest to come by because it requires a leap of faith on the part of the buyer. You should try to make that leap as much of a baby step as possible, but it still means buyers has to put their faith and trust in you to deliver exactly what was promised in your ad.

Once the item is received and it's exactly what was expected, the buyer immediately feels good about the whole experience. With just one positive experience, your stock increases considerably as the buyer associates positive feelings towards you. If you've got something else to offer that this particular buyer is interested in, you've got a much better shot at winning him or her over a second time.

The problem is that unless your buyers constantly monitor your new listings, they won't know about the other products you offer. That's why it's important to build a mailing list and keep in touch with your marketplace periodically. Specialize in a specific category and then create an opt-in form on your About Me page, so buyers in one subject area can be notified of new listings as you post them.

You'll have to be careful in your approach with this strategy. Everyone online is affected by unwanted emails, so use a 'spaced repetition' strategy and only send messages when you've got something new or different to offer. Remember: the whole idea is to further endear customers to you, making them more likely to buy again and again. You can't achieve this ideal however if you pester people too frequently.

Allow anyone who signs up to opt-out easily and instantly. Let your subscribers know they're in full control. You'd like them to stay onboard, but they're totally free to do whatever they wish at anytime. And vow to keep their information (email address) strictly to yourself.

Buyers get a feeling about you – positive or negative – through every transaction. They make a judgment call that can either help your enterprise grow long term, or kill it in a heartbeat. Your goal should always be to create happy buyers who are delighted to leave you positive feedback. Shoot for this lofty ideal with the best of intentions and you'll reach it most of the time.

# Chapter Eight: Photo Basics

Photos are important on eBay because most of us are visual in nature. When we think, we think in pictures. If we see it with our own eyes, we tend to accept it as real much more readily. But the opposite is also true. What we cannot see, we tend to question.

An image captures various bits of information and formulates it into something concrete and visual – something that can be understood at a glance. A photo attached to an eBay listing tells all exactly what is being offered and this information is processed instantaneously.

Without a clear, descriptive photo, it's difficult to get a good handle on an item. Mental images are still created, but they could differ dramatically from what is actually up for sale.

## Visual Detail Builds Confidence

Clear, detailed, even dramatic photographs can seriously increase the perceived value of your items. They help your prospective buyers gain a better understanding of what it is that you're actually selling and they drive prices upward. Most importantly, a quality photo delivers a realistic expectation, so buyers can be comfortable with what they're bidding on before actually placing a bid.

Since most people are visual, they're drawn towards visual images. That's what makes a Gallery Image (that small thumbnail snapshot of your product that is displayed next to the Title) so important.

Images that are interesting or dramatic for one reason or another and used as Gallery shots, tend to capture the largest audiences. Simple eye-appeal is the reason. Your listing, complete with an effective image next to the title, blows others away that were listed without the up-front visual aid of a clear picture.

Gallery photographs work in tandem with your title to grab eyeballs and capture interest. A strong title may do the job on its own. But it's usually more effective when combined with a clear and unique photograph that speaks volumes to the interested prospective buyer.

This is the one added-cost option I strongly recommend. Rarely do I list an item without also using a Gallery Image. It's an added feature that costs a bit more, but it's well worth it in my opinion. But even if you choose not to use a Gallery photo due to the extra cost involved, you'd be foolhardy not to include at least one photo with your listing as the first one is free. For subsequent shots (up to 5 more) -- eBay charges an additional fee.

## Don't List Any Item Without At Least One Photo

It makes no sense to list anything – even items of the least imaginable value – without the benefit of a photograph. A photo communicates important information to your potential buyer. And the first one in each listing is free. So it makes absolutely no sense to create a listing without an image of some kind.

If you do list without the benefit of photographs, you can expect to sell fewer items, attract only minimal bids, and be avoided altogether by many experienced buyers who won't even consider an item they can't get a quick visual on.

## The Only 3 Things You Really Need

You don't need an elaborate and expensive set-up in order to take effective photos that help to sell your goods on eBay.

All you really need are these basics...

1) **Natural light...**
2) **A suitable camera...** and...
3) **Something to display your item on.**

Just keep it simple and it's much easier to kick into action whenever you're ready.

Almost any camera will do to get you started on eBay. But as you progress by listing more items and making more money, you'll probably want to upgrade your equipment. Not only does a quality digital camera give you better images, it makes life a whole lot easier for you.

Ideally, a camera and scanner gives you everything you need to create great quality images at any time. You may be wondering why I even mentioned a scanner with the dramatic improvements in digital photography. Well, for most three-dimensional items, a decent camera is all you need.

But if you want to capture superb quality images of flat items like book covers, postage stamps, or comic books, a scanner may be even more valuable than the best camera. The reason is that a good scanner delivers a more consistent visual representation because the lighting is set perfectly. Leave it to your own devices and unless you're a pro or photography buff, you probably won't get an image that's as clear and crisp as the one your trusty scanner can produce.

If you're shopping for a digital camera, look for one with at least 3-4 megapixels. This will give you clear images, rather than fuzzy ones. For the first few years of my eBay business, I used a 1.3 megapixel camera. This was among the best available at the time. But when I finally upgraded to a 5 megapixel unit -- the difference in clarity and crispness was obvious.

Another important consideration is how the camera stores images. I much prefer those with portable storage cards as this gives me plenty of storage space, an easy way to upload images to my computer, and flexibility between computers.

Most of the cheaper digital cameras don't have this feature. Instead, all images are recorded to the camera's own internal memory. If your camera goes down, you may find it difficult or expensive to retrieve your images. But when your images are recorded on a portable memory card like Compact Flash or Secure Digital, you simply remove the card and you're good to go. You can then upload your images anytime you want.

It is possible to get product shots without having a camera. For some items, stock photos can be used. Even clip art or simple line drawings can work too, instead of a photograph.

Some eBay information product sellers prefer this to a photo, since their items are often downloadable, rather than physical. Another option is to use a scanner for flat items like collectable postage stamps, maps, small posters, or historical documents.

Put yourself in your buyer's shoes. You're asking them to make a buying decision from afar. They can't see the item with their own eyes. They can't touch it, hold it, or gain the perspective of having this physical item before them. So your best bet is to help out with detailed photographs that accurately represent the item being offered.

Next, you need to find some workspace.

Start with a clear tabletop or work surface. If you can devote a corner of a room and set up your own little studio, that's even better. But if you can't create a designated area, that's okay. But what you absolutely must have is a clear table to place your items on – one at a time.

A table is far superior to a desk for one simple reason: clutter is less likely to accumulate on a table as opposed to a desk. If you have to take time to clean off your desk every time you set out to get a few items listed, you'll waste valuable time and energy that could otherwise be spent getting more stuff listed. The result is you'll list fewer things and make less money.

## A Suitable Background

Okay… so you've got a camera and a table. What's needed next is some background material. Any solid material (not patterned) is good and if it's white in color, so much the better. I've used white linen as a backdrop for some larger items like vases and old movie projectors and it worked well. For smaller items like mp3 players and books, I simply use a flat sheet of white Bristol board laid out on the table.

For the majority of items, white makes a good background. It allows the item to be presented as the main feature, rather than competing with something else. Busy backgrounds distract viewers from what they really should be looking at. It's the item you want to sell, not the props. So it's best to make your background as "invisible" as you can. In other words, don't draw attention to anything other than the item. A plain, nondescript, white background is ideal for most items.

Occasionally, another color used as the background is more effective than white. I just listed a hardcover book that was almost all white, with some bright blue and red lettering. It didn't look so good on a white background, but on a midnight blue background, it really stood out.

## Adequate Lighting

Lighting is one of the major keys to taking great product shots. I've found that it's best to have two separate overhead lights that can be adjusted to accommodate the change in natural lighting throughout the day. Halogen track lights work well as the light they shine is whiter and brighter than that from standard incandescent bulbs.

Another option is to set up your temporary photo studio outdoors. If you live in an area where it's warm year-round, this is easy to do. If not, you'll probably want to do this seasonally. Just take your table and sheet and move it outside to a shaded area. Avoid taking shots in direct sunlight. On a bright sunny day, many shaded areas are excellent for capturing quality product shots. Look for consistent shading. Then, just set up your portable studio and snap a whole bunch of items in quick succession. Working in stages like this can save you a lot of time overall.

## eBay Photo Basics

If you want to create as many effective eBay listings as you can in as little time as possible, remember to keep things simple. There's just no need for anything too involved, elaborate, or complicated. Efficiency is the name of the game.

Make your item the star of the show. Put the spotlight on each product you want to list. A plain background that isn't the least bit distracting won't compete for your prospect's attention, making it easy to put the product front and center.

Use natural light as much as possible as it delivers uniformity and clarity. It's easy to attain – just go outside. Sure, you may be somewhat limited by weather conditions. But when conditions are perfect, you can set up your outdoor studio and snap a couple of week's worth of items for your listings. Lighting is a major key to getting good product shots. If you're a novice photographer like me, you can save yourself a lot of hassle by setting up your studio outdoors.

## Make It Sparkle

Clean the item before capturing the image. This might seem obvious, but you'd be surprised how many sellers overlook the obvious.

It's not just eBay sellers that make this mistake either. I've often discovered merchandise in stores – even food items that were dusty or had something spilled on them at some point that was never cleaned. For some people, (sellers and buyers) a little dirt might not matter. But if it costs you one bidder, it's money down the drain.

Used items are particularly susceptible. You wouldn't sell your used car without cleaning it first, would you? If you did, you'd surely be throwing money away. So take the time to clean those items before taking your snapshots. But do so with care – particularly with delicate, collectible, or antique items. It's best to avoid harsh chemicals as a general rule. But that's no reason not to clean.

## Upload Your Images

After you've taken shots of several items, it's time to upload them to your computer. It's important at this point to do some minor photo-editing before posting your shots with your listings. You need to make some adjustments to your images to polish them up before including them in your ads.

To make those changes, you'll need a software program designed for photo manipulation to carry out these simple steps. Most digital cameras sold these days come with free photo-editing software included. You can also find some free programs online. One that I like is called *Irfanview* and you can find it at irfanview.com

## How To Improve Any Image At Zero Cost

If you have your own photo-editing software installed and you're quite comfortable using it and you're happy with the results, by all means, continue doing what you're doing. And if you've got Photoshop installed, you're one step ahead as it's the ultimate program in photo-manipulation. Photoshop is the expert's tool of choice for photo editing. But putting a program like this to effective use usually requires some training as there's a definite learning curve involved. With adequate training and practice, you can create masterpieces of stunning beauty.

But to make money as an eBay Seller, you really don't need to be a professional photographer and you don't need Photoshop to deliver images that get the job done. Irfanview enables you to enhance your images in no time at all and it won't cost you a thing. It's "freeware" so you never have to worry about paying a fee for its use.

What I love about *Irfanview* is that it's so easy to use. I usually make 3 basic adjustments to my images and then they're good to go. Those 3 steps are cropping, adjusting the brightness and contrast, and resizing the image.

Just launch the program and then open one image at a time. Make your adjustments and then name the file so you can find it easily later when you go to write your listing.

As you open an image, the first thing you'll notice is that it's much larger than it needs to be. Simply change the view by zooming out. To do this, click the magnifying glass icon with the minus symbol inside. If you look at the toolbar across the top of the window, you'll see two magnifying glasses – a plus for zooming in and a minus for zooming out. Click the one on the right a number of times in succession to zoom out until your view of the image is at a comfortable and workable size. You haven't done anything to the image itself at this point. All you've done is adjust what you see on the screen.

The next step is to crop the image. That's where you simply frame the item itself and cut away the excess. It's where you take your imaginary scissors and cut around the item and discard the rest. It cleans up the image and makes your item the star of the show. You don't need the extra background anyway. Cropping your pictures this way is like trimming tops and peeling fresh carrots. You cut off the waste so that all you're left with is usable goods.

Next, proceed to the Image Menu, and then scroll down the list to Enhance Colors. Here you're presented with a simple, sliding scale adjustment for both the brightness and contrast.

I usually increase both to varying degrees. Just slide the arrow along the bar and watch the changes made to the image above on the right. This is the modified version while the one on the left is the original. When you've got your image looking the way you want, click OK.

The final steps are to resize your image, name it, and save it to your eBay file.

Go to the Image Menu again. This time you're looking for the Resize/Resample tab. Click on it and you'll see the current size of your image. The one I'm working on now shows a width of 2592 pixels and a Height of 1944 pixels. This is way too big for my purposes on eBay. The largest dimension shouldn't be any more than 600 - 700 pixels, so I simply adjust the width of my image accordingly.

When I change it to 600 pixels, it automatically adjusts the Height in perfect proportion. So my image is now 600 pixels wide and 450 pixels high. The feature that allowed me to preserve the original image proportions is the "Preserve Aspect Ratio" button in the Resize/Resample window. My image is now the ideal size for eBay. All I have to do at this point is proceed to the File Menu, scroll down to Save As and enter a name, and then click the Save button. That's all there is to it.

It's best to save your images as jpeg files as it works well whether you use eBay's Picture Services or host the images on your own web space.

A tripod can make your life a whole lot easier. Without any movement of your hands to worry about, you'll get cleaner, more focused pictures without fuzzy edges. If you're doing lots of similarly-sized items like jewelry or dinner plates, you can set up your camera on a tripod and arrange things just right. Then, simply change the item each time. Set it up for the best possible shot once… and then you can do any number of similar items without having to change anything.

Use pictures that talk. You want your image to reveal as much detail about the item as possible. But sometimes you just can't do that effectively with a single shot, so having multiple images is often helpful. If using multiple shots, try showing your item in action, or at least in an appropriate room setting. Have someone model footwear, jewelry, or clothing. Or have your model smile while holding the item in front of them.

Expose details of importance like the manufacturer's name stamped on the back of your collectible dinner plate, or the number affixed that reveals the limited release of a Robert Bateman print. That's the kind of detail that legitimizes the claims you make in your ad copy.

Reveal a product advantage in your photograph. For example, if you want to sell a collectible GI Joe set that's been stored away in your attic for the past 35 years, show the original packaging in your picture. Not only does it help authenticate your age claim, but it also adds perceived value by proving that the product is still in its original box.

Another way to accomplish an advantage is to show your product in use. A Vita mix machine shown in the process of whipping up a delicious Strawberry-Pineapple Smoothie, illustrates one of the many things it can do and it proves to the prospect that this high-powered kitchen device actually works.

If you're selling an old portable stereo and it happens to be a major brand and made in Japan, show that specific detail (even though it's printed only on the back) as it could mean a significant difference in profits earned.

Make the item the focal point. It's the only component of the photograph that matters to prospective buyers. Bring it to the forefront. Expose it as best you can. Reveal its age, condition, brand, origin, and any other important detail you can think of. Show as much detail as you can in your pictures and then make sure your copy is in perfect harmony so each element supports the other, rather than oppose it.

## Creating Even Better Images

Photography is a learned skill. Thanks to technology, you don't have to know much about cameras to take effective product shots these days. And better photos help you sell items at higher prices on eBay. But the more you get to know your equipment and what it takes to capture great product shots, the greater your chances of making more money when your auctions close.

There's no better way to improve a learned skill than through practice. Practice makes improvement. Just be willing to try new things and see how they turn out. You can always get better at taking pictures. But you certainly don't need to be any kind of an expert to create effective eBay item shots.

Learn by watching what other sellers do. Regularly check out other auctions – not just those in the categories you prefer – but in as many different areas of eBay as you can. Take note of what others do and simply apply what works.

For example, I noticed one seller offering handcrafted denim handbags. But what really stood out was how they were displayed. It wasn't just a plain old handbag sitting lifelessly on a table. This seller showed off her wares by showing them in use by a model. The bag was the star of the show, but the human element certainly set her images apart from most of the others in that category. Is there a way to inject some human interest into your product images? If so, give it a shot. You may find your upgraded image helps improve your results.

## Use Multiple Pictures

Only your first image is free. Anything over and above that will cost you extra money. But, depending on your item, the small added costs may be well worth the investment. The trick is to show your item as explicitly as possible. You need to make it clear exactly what the winning bidder receives and sometimes that's difficult to do with just a single shot.

Use multiple photographs to show...

- Every element or various key components of your entire package...

- The offer in its entirety, different ways or from different angles...

148

- The rewards or results obtained from the main product (if you're selling grass seed, show a lush green lawn)...

- The product in action...

- A more interesting shot of your item...

- A human element, such as smiling faces enjoying the product...

- Different close-up views to clearly reveal important details or markings...

- Specific damage done to the item...

Believability is important to the success of your listings. This applies to both written copy and visual images. If it looks too far-fetched, it won't be accepted. Only use photographs that add to your sales presentation. Eliminate all others prior to posting.

## How To Convey Your Item's Actual Size and Color

Here's a trick I learned from my friend, Terry Gibbs in his book, *The Auction Revolution*. The idea is to insert something into your image that everyone can relate to, in order to add clarity to the item itself.

In other words, if I was listing a small pocket timer, I might add a piece of popcorn and place it beside the timer. What this does is eliminate any confusion as to the size of the item being featured. Everyone knows the approximate size of a piece of popcorn. There may be slight variations, but not enough to make an inaccurate conclusion as to the size of the timer.

If I wanted to be more precise, perhaps a coin such as a quarter would be better, or a standard credit card. The idea is to provide a reference point, so potential buyers can quickly determine the over all size, relative to something they instinctively know.

Terry takes this one step further. He's an expert at selling collectible train sets. In this world of the serious collector, color is very important. Short runs and limited edition colors fetch a premium because they're rare. What Terry does when he's selling a red train is this: he places a can of Coca-Cola® next to the item.

I suspect that very few people on the planet, if any, don't have an internal recognition for the color of "Coke® red". So instantly this reference point provides a measuring stick. This can be extremely helpful in certain situations. The size of the can is also a good gauge as typical soda pop cans are a standard size.

Other items you could use as size and/or color gauges are pens, dollar bills, regular coins, coffee cups, clearly marked rulers, measuring cups, or popsicle sticks. If it doesn't help convey accurate information, it probably doesn't belong in your image. Some brands that have distinctive colors on their logos or product packaging include *Coca-Cola, Pepsi, Canada Dry Ginger Ale, Campbell's Soup, Krispy Kreme, etc.*

The only time you'll want to include any prop in addition to your item is when using a point of reference adds clarity and precise detail for the prospect. Anything else should be considered a distraction that focuses attention away from the item you intend to sell.

## How To Make The Best Use Of Your Time

On eBay, you make money two ways:

*1) You make money when you acquire solid, in-demand merchandise at a great price so you have an automatic, built-in profit and...*

*2) You make money by creating powerful ads that sell and getting them posted.*

The more deals you can find and the more quality listings you can get uploaded, the wider and deeper your marketing reach and the greater your profit potential. These two activities are critical to making more money on eBay. Everything else is secondary in importance.

But as we've already noted, your images are one of the three main factors in every eBay ad you post. So, there's no corner-cutting here. You need the best, most descriptive pictures that talk to prospects and help pull them inside. But the photograph element need not be a time consuming task.

To save time, have several items nearby, ready to be captured on camera. If you do it one at a time, it will take all day to add a significant number of listings on eBay. You don't need a huge number – I like to take my snapshots and write my ads in lots of ten. But you should work with a quantity that you're most comfortable in handling.

It's important to only take photographs of the items you plan to list that day. If you let it go, eventually, you'll have so many images that you've forgotten about altogether. Consequently, you'll end up wasting time trying to locate these later, or by re-shooting them needlessly.

If you've got a permanent studio set up in the corner of a room, it's not much trouble to go back and forth from studio to computer. But once you're set up and ready to roll, it makes more sense to capture the images of at least a half a dozen different products in one session.

Grouping a bunch of photographs together makes good use of your time. I don't recommend doing too many at once, or you may find yourself exhausted before you're even ready to create descriptive ad copy to sell your items. As you make a regular habit of this and you continue to increase your skill and proficiency, there's nothing wrong with challenging yourself to go one step further and increase capacity. But remember, the image is just one element and you need all three (image, title, and description) and then they must be activated on eBay to make you any money.

Do it in stages. Set up your studio and take one shot after another. Once you've done a manageable number, proceed to the next step, which is to upload these images from your camera to your computer. It just doesn't make sense to do it one image at a time.

If you've captured your photos on a memory card, it's quick and easy to do. Just remove the memory card from your camera and insert it into your computer's card reader and follow the steps on the screen. Just be sure to record your eBay images in a separate file so you know exactly where they are when you need them.

If your images are stored on your camera's internal memory, it means digging out the cable and connecting to your computer that way. It's still pretty easy to do. I prefer using memory cards though as they're a quick and easy solution.

Once you've got all your images on your computer's hard drive, it's time to edit them. Again, it's just plain inefficient to do one and then move onto the next phase. Edit every photograph in your group and then name each for easy retrieval. If you took 6 item shots today, you should have also uploaded those 6 images and it only makes sense to edit the same 6 in one fell swoop before proceeding. Get comfortable with this and you'll find your ability to handle progressively larger numbers increasingly easy.

Take actions in sequence and you'll accomplish much more in less time. The real stars on eBay spend a lot less time on their businesses than you might think. They've learned to become masters of efficiency, so they get to spend more time doing whatever they want, while their ads are up on eBay attracting attention and action.

# <u>Chapter Nine</u>: Using Long Copy To Sell On eBay

The Golden Formula For Selling On eBay
The Complete Sales Letter
7 Steps To Sales Letter Success

When your potential profit warrants it, expand on these ideas to provide even more detail, more advantages, and more enticements. The way to do this is with a sales letter approach.

There's one reason why the sales letter is the tool of choice for most copywriters: it works exceptionally well in converting prospects into buyers.

Sales letters provide unlimited space to make your best possible sales proposition. They're particularly effective when selling information products or software – when there's not shortage of details to cover.

You might choose a sales letter approach when selling anything of higher value such as a website, or a business. When it pays to do so, structure your ad into a compelling sales letter.

You could formulate your sales letter using the AIDA method discussed earlier. There are several other step-by-step methods to crafting a letter *(More examples of effective sales letter strategies from top ad writers can be found in the book - Winning Website Sales Letters).*

You might also find the upcoming formula to be very effective in the auction marketplace.

## The Golden Formula For Selling On eBay

Use this as you see fit in your eBay ads. You'll notice it's an evolutionary development of the AIDA formula that goes a few steps beyond the original version. You could apply this formula to a half-page ad format or a multi-page sales letter.

1. Capture Your Best Prospect's Attention (Same as step one above)

2. Reveal Why He or She Should Be VERY Interested In Your Listing (What do you have for your target prospect? What's in it for him?)

3. Tell Why Your Prospect Should Believe You (Who are you and how does your personal history, experience, or chance encounter make you someone he should listen to)

4. Prove It (Show pictures, share your story, cite examples, provide test results, or supply customer testimonials)

5. List the Benefits of your Item and Briefly Describe Each (Bullet Points work well here)

6. Declare All Relevant Facts and Features (Brand, model, size, color, age, condition, packaging, previous owner, damages, etc.)

7. Emphasize Your Track Record of Exceptional Customer Service and Quick Shipping (Ease their fears about doing business with someone they don't yet know)

8. Nudge Prospects To ACTION Now (Remind them that it's in their best interest to do so. Give them a valid reason to act now rather than to put it off)

## The Complete Sales Letter

A well written sales letter can sell anything and in huge quantities. Pound for pound, there's no more powerful direct response sales tool. It's the ultimate weapon for attracting targeted prospects, building an interesting proposition, fueling desire for your product, and for influencing action. A sales letter is an excellent opportunity to apply the AIDA formula, the Golden formula for selling on eBay, or any one of dozens of tested advertising methods.

The sales letter is the polar opposite to the compact classified ad. At minimum, a sales letter is one page long -- but it could stretch 25 or 30 pages – or even longer. The thing about a sales letter on eBay is that you can take all the space you need to present your most appealing and persuasive case.

You can add even more benefits... include additional customer testimonials... bundle multiple products into your offer... do a price comparison chart with competing products... use additional case histories... and so on. You're not limited in any way. But that doesn't give you free reign to chatter either. Stay on course and focus on selling.

Only add words that contribute to your sales presentation and make it as interesting to the reader as possible. Regardless of its length, every ad has to command the attention of your target customers through to the end -- or it fails. So if you're adding multiple pages, you better make sure it's interesting to the prospect. If it doesn't contribute, it doesn't belong.

Most everyday items and even the one-of-a-kind pieces people sell on eBay, don't require or justify, a sales letter. Sales letters can eat up a lot of time getting them just right. So you want to be sure your potential profit makes the time investment seem reasonable.

If you buy large quantities of identical goods by the pallet, it's probably worth your while to create a strong sales letter. But selling in ones or twos means you should likely resort to one of the quicker methods for writing eBay ad listings.

If you're selling your own information products such as books, CD's or DVD's – a sales letter can help you sell items week after week, for years. And if you've got the reprint or duplication rights to other products, you could potentially market these for a long time to come, though your competition would likely be greater. So a sales letter might be viable here. But if you're selling the same kind of individual information products you've previously owned, or those you've acquired for resale, you'd probably be better off creating shorter ads and adding multiple listings.

If your situation justifies using sales letters, than by all means, do so. But get a handle on your profit potential first, before investing hours in a killer letter-style listing.

What I love about writing sales letters is they provide an opportunity to write with passion and enthusiasm and to infuse sales copy with emotion. Emotion sells. So the more enthusiasm you can generate, the more you sell.

Sales letters give you the chance to create compelling offers that are difficult, if not impossible to resist. When you're selling information products that you won the rights to, it's easy to create additional bonuses with high perceived values. And often it's the right mix of bonus offers that can sway an uncertain prospect and convince him to move forward at once.

Whether you write a lengthy sales letter or a condensed ad of half a page or so, you need to appeal to those who are interested. You've got to target this market and forget about trying to please anyone else. You need to know who is best for your item because even the best copy written by the world's greatest copywriter will flop if you're trying to sell to the wrong market. To the wrong market, half a page is far too long. But the right market will read multiple pages – as long as these prospects are brimming with interest.

Don't make your ads longer than they need to be. But don't leave out a single point of interest to your target buyer either. A lot of people think nobody would bother to read a long sales letter. But when readers are intensely interested in your offer, they'll not only read every word, but many will follow through and place a bid.

The easiest way to craft a letter is to stick to a formula of some kind. You've learned about AIDA and the Golden formula and I've added another just below. Each formula in itself could be used to create powerful sales letters you could use successfully on eBay.

It doesn't really matter which one you choose, though with some experience, you'll tend to favor one or two over the others. Just follow your chosen system through step-by-step and you'll have the basis of a solid sales letter. Then, continue to massage and edit your sales copy into a powerful, persuasive piece that flows effortlessly.

## 7 Steps To Sales Letter Success

Here's a 7-step formula to create an effective sales letter.

> **1. Capture Your Best Prospect's <u>Attention</u>.** Use your title and Gallery image to woo potential buyers to your full Item Description. Give them the information they want and need to qualify themselves as prospects. If you're selling black leather jackets, you need to let people know early that your jackets are available in black only. This disqualifies those looking for brown, beige, blue, purple or any other color.
>
> Deliver the words that would most interest a buyer and make a big promise. "Promise, large promise is the soul of an advertisement" said British author, Samuel Johnson back in the 1700's. And he was right. Making a big promise is just as effective today on eBay.

There are numerous ways to create headlines to launch into your full-scale sales pitch. But the easiest way to unveil the big promise of your item is to lead with the time-tested "How To" headline approach. Start with "How To" – and just add an appealing promise that your product can help the buyer get, enjoy, achieve, or profit from.

**2. Reveal Why Your Prospect Should Be <u>Interested</u> In Your Advertisement.** Expand on the promise of your headline. Create a vivid image of the desired results. Paint a glorious picture by having them imagine what it's going to be like to own your item, to use it, to enjoy it, to be able to treasure it, profit from it, or pass it along as a family keepsake.

It's important to put your potential buyer in the picture. In order to buy, they need to feel the advantages of doing so. And in order to feel it, they have to be able to see the picture in their mind.

Get them enthused enough, and the pleasurable images will consume them. But don't hesitate to get the ball rolling by encouraging prospects to "Imagine that" or to "Picture this in your mind's eye". Allow them to mentally entertain the idea and the corresponding benefits will invariably shine through. Sell the dream, not the item.

**3. Make Yours A <u>Rare</u> Offering.** People in general and eBayers specifically love original, rare, or unique items and packages. Therefore, you want your particular offer to stand out and be extra special when compared to anything similar. Instead of offering a product, make it a package. Add unique value with extra bonuses. Information products make excellent bonuses for just about any item you want to sell in quantities. Once you've created it, it's simply a matter of duplication. It's the information itself that holds value. Create a package deal that's exclusively yours. That way your prospects simply cannot get the same thing anywhere else.

**4. Explain How The <u>Buyer</u> Comes Out On Top.** Pile on the benefits. Let them know what they get as a result of owning the item. Create a list of one valuable advantage after another. Set them up as powerful bullet points so prospects can quickly grasp the main benefits and move on quickly.

Write your bullet points like headlines. Simply preface each big benefit with a phrase like these, or something similar...

- 3 Little-Known Ways To...

- A Simple, 3-Minute Solution To...

- The Amazing Secret Of...

- How To...

- In Less Than 5 Minutes, You Can...

- Easy Steps To...

- Advice Pros Give To...

- 5 Insider Techniques To...

- Common Mistakes That Actually Reverse Results...

- Why 99%...

- The Dirty Little Secret To...

**5. Introduce Your Irresistible <u>Offer</u>.** Create as stark a contrast as possible between what the item/package is worth versus how little you're asking in return. This is where a low starting bid can instantly create a flurry of activity.

Give them dollars worth of value for mere pennies. Thanks to the auction-style, bid-what-you-want format of eBay, it's easy to offer genuine value at bargain-basement prices, without raising suspicions. After all, you expect the price to go much higher. But it's awfully tempting for prospects to simply go for it.

**6. <u>Prove</u> What You Said Is True.** Provide customer testimonials and case histories whenever possible. Legitimate third party endorsements can go a long way in convincing prospects of your selling points. Look at the way products are sold in infomercials today. A large chunk of the total airtime is devoted to customers telling their stories.

If you say it, it may be looked upon as mere advertising. But when a previous customer tells a compelling story of satisfaction with your product, it's perceived as much closer to the truth.

Whenever possible, give buyers a satisfaction guarantee. And the longer, the better.

**7. Seal The Deal and Close The <u>Sale</u>.** Your sales letter only works if it leads to action. Don't leave prospects half-sold on your item. Give them that extra nudge. Direct them to take action and provide a clear reason why it's in their best interest to do so NOW.

Remind them of the great deal you have to offer. Summarize all they get from you. Make it worth far more than even the regular price of your package. And since you're only asking for a much lower Buy-It-Now price, or a tiny starting bid, taking action should be a no-brainer.

Tell your prospects exactly what they need to do to get all the benefits for themselves... make taking the necessary action easy to do.

# Chapter Ten: Creating Titles That Grab Attention

Your Title Is The #1 Key To Great Results
What Works Best?
Start With Key Product Information
How To Get Maximum Mileage From Your Title
Some Examples of Effective Titles Key Title Concepts
3 Steps To Creating A Powerful Title That Attracts Attention
More Quick and Easy Title Tips

## Your Title Is The #1 Key To Great Results

Nothing is more important to each individual listing than the title that leads it. In fact, your overall success on eBay is dependent to a large degree on your ability to create effective headlines that pull in large amounts of quality traffic. It's the title that's the key to capturing the attention and interest of your target market.

Your title is your initial point of contact. It's the first thing any shopper on eBay sees with respect to your individual auction.

If a prospective buyer conducts a 'keyword search' -- as approximately 70% of eBayers do -- your keyword-specific listing may be one of hundreds, or even thousands of listings that are shown. So your title needs to have the associated word or phrase to show up on a search for that term. But it also needs to be compelling enough to win clicks and get your listing opened by more interested prospects.

Your title is just as important to shoppers who choose to peruse listings in their favorite categories. Here your ad has to appear more interesting than the others. Even devout shoppers only have so much available time. Nobody looks at everything. Instead, they tend to zero in on the things that most interest them -- in the moment. So your title or headline has to grab hearts and minds instantly.

If your title fails, the rest of your ad description is insignificant. If they don't click on the title, they won't go to your page immediately. And if they miss it in the moment, 99.9% of browsers won't even think of coming back. There's just too much to explore on eBay and one search invariably leads to another.

You've only got limited space. Currently, eBay gives you a maximum of 55 characters to use any way you like in the Title field. It's not a lot of space... so you have to choose your words and abbreviated forms with great care.

Titles are all about attracting the eyes of targeted prospects enough to get them to at least visit your more detailed description. If they don't go beyond the title, they cannot bid, Buy-It-Now, ask you a question about the item, or your terms, or even sign up to your mailing list. All those actions require that they at least land on an individual auction description page and the most valuable tool you have to achieve this is your Title.

Every listing has a Title. Most also feature a Gallery Image, which is an added-cost option, but one that's almost always worth it in the end. Gallery Images and Titles are what show up in any list, whether that list was derived from a keyword search or by scanning an individual sub-category.

Gallery Images are always shown alongside their corresponding Titles. It's a one-two punch that almost always attracts more clicks than listings that don't use the Gallery Image option and have to rely on the straight text of their Titles.

You've got one small box to fill with just 55 characters, including spaces. If you try to jam in too much at the expense of a space, you only create more problems for yourself. Combined words won't show up in searches, unless the one doing the search happens to choose the exact same combination. What's more, your jumbled character creation might look more like a foreign language than a smart, keyword-stuffed combination. This could easily negate your attempts to squeeze in more detail and firepower.

The only "tools" you have available for use in the Title Field are the individual letters of the alphabet and your ability to think creatively. It's imperative that you choose what brings the most value or uniqueness to your offering and do so in a way that's most likely to strike a chord with the largest number of potential bidders.

For example, if you're listing a pair of ladies shoes, style, brand, and condition are all important. But nothing is more important than the size – as far as shoe sales go. Nobody buys a size that doesn't fit the person they're intended for. If you fail to reveal the size in your Title, you'll attract fewer page views, unless the shoes you're selling are from a celebrity and being sold as a collectible. In that case, size probably doesn't matter, except to validate your claims.

Select your words with care. Try several combinations before settling on the one you think will bring you the most traffic.

Strive to be descriptive while making an impact at the same time. Whatever words you choose will be quickly consumed by busy shoppers in search of treasures. Deliver these few words within your Title and they're quickly gobbled up and processed and a decision is made. Often this process takes only a second or two and even less for the scanning reader. You've only got a moment to make an impact. The decision is made -- for or against. Viewers click through to your description, or they carry on and most of the time, this decision is made instantaneously.

Make enough of an impact to get your Title noticed and acted upon. That's what you want to do with every listing. The key job of the Title is to attract interested prospects and welcome them inside. Remember that most people who see your Title are serious buyers and not just window shopping. Your objective is to get the click and that responsibility falls for the most part on your title.

## What Works Best?

Your optimum Title strategy will vary according to the item and category you're listing. For example, for something like a handbag, the brand name or designer label might be most important. But if you were to list a book on self-confidence, your best bet might be to stress the advantage offered over the title and author, unless the author had a well-developed "brand" like a Wayne Dyer or Deepak Chopra.

With a collectible such as a grandfather clock, what could be most significant about yours? Perhaps it's the year it was made, the specific model, the craftsman who designed/built it, or the fact that in that year only, a different chime was used, making it a rare piece. Avid collectors seek unique and rare pieces and will often pay higher prices.

An easy way to get started with a great title is to take the list below and simply fill in the blanks. List all that applies to your particular item.

## Start With Key Product Information

Item:
Brand/Author/Designer:
Model:
Year Made:
Title:
Style:
Size:
Color:
Condition:
Packaging:

Once you've identified the basics of your item, it's time to decide on those items that are most important to your particular listing. You'll want to include as many of these specifics as possible in your Title.

Remember, you only have 55 characters of space, so choose wisely. You'll also want to consider using short-forms, for example – "09" rather than "2009" if you were selling something normally referenced by year of make or release such as cars, figurines, or even MP3 players. Every space saved is a valuable piece of real estate you can use in another way. Just be sure not to shorten or compress words to the point where they're unintelligible.

In addition to these key product references, you'll get better results when you inject sales power into your title. One technique I've used successfully is to target your ideal prospect within your title. Think of it as calling out to those specific people who would be most interested in your item. For example, you might inject the word "Gardeners" to your auction listing for an audio CD of an interview with an expert on the topic. A directory of wholesale suppliers for the jewelry making business could attract more visitors by calling out to "jewelers" right in the title.

Now before you claim that this is completely unnecessary because after all, the category you're listing in should make it apparent who your ad is directed toward, think again. Most Sellers in your category probably don't use this technique because they think this way. But picture if you will, your prospect scanning hundreds of different listings in a category. Only a few will jump out and grab his attention. If this prospect clearly belongs to your prospect group, an ad addressed specifically to that group is music to his hears. He simply cannot by-pass your ad in favor of another because it's as if someone has called out to him by name.

People take great pride in their associations and interests. Therefore, any title that targets a specific association or special interest group tends to attract the eyes of more targeted prospects than those titles that don't. There are just so many ads on eBay that most users are half asleep consciously, even when searching for the very things they most want.

How can this be? Well, most of what they find, in fact, the huge majority of listings could be of absolutely no interest to the prospect at this time. So he skims along at breakneck speed, trusting his eyes to scope out only the items with a high degree of relevancy.

When your title speaks to this specific individual as a mechanic, parent, animal lover, or hemorrhoid sufferer – any one of a million different "identifiers" – you're speaking his language and are by default, much more likely to get a hearing. It's an old direct response trick gleaned from the masters of advertising. It's something I often see being used on eBay. But it does work.

There's one more category of words I like to use in titles wherever possible. I simply refer to these as "Power Words". Power words are those that add a little sales punch to your 60-character lead description. They're used to give your listing an added push or advantage over another offering the same or similar items. Unfortunately, many Sellers get caught up in the selling game and misuse or over-use them, diminishing their power for all of us. But they can still work well when used appropriately and effectively.

Power words include such gems as: rare (one of my favorites), gift, free bonus, free shipping, guaranteed, sale, exciting, and no reserve. Your aim is to get the click BEFORE the next guy. So any added advantage or extra enticement can help sway more action your way.

## How To Get Maximum Mileage From Your Title

If you've never written a listing before, facing the limitation of 55 characters for your title can be a little stifling. (*eBay has since upped this limitation to 80 characters. But if you master the 55-

character title – you'll find it easy to add additional details to suit.) It always helps to remember that every advertiser faces the same challenge you do.

We're all limited to the same number, single color, and the fact that it's a text-only field. The only real options are for a bold or featured listing. These ads run at the top of any list and are therefore subjected to more eyeballs in the process. It's a way of gaining something by paying to rank higher in order. It may be worth your consideration to test these two options and determine whether they helped improve your profits.

There is one free option that can help your headline stand out in any list, and it is simply this: the correct use of capitalization.

Some advertisers use almost all lowercase text. Others prefer all UPPERCASE. Neither in my view is the best option in any environment. Lowercase test seems rather uninteresting and ordinary, like it's just one line from a full page of text. It tends to blend in, rather than stand out.

Uppercase text, on the other hand, can be likened to standing on a busy street corner and screaming at the top of your lungs. It's not exactly the best way to attract people to your message.

There's already too much "noise" we all have to deal with daily. Any more of the same quickly shuts down an otherwise interested mind. Uppercase text is also more difficult to read. And although the title field is only 55 characters, it still requires extra time to read and comprehend the meaning of those words.

But uppercase characters can be very effective when used sparingly.

The best method I've found is to capitalize the first character of each word. If you were to study the most successful ads, sales letters and web pages, in virtually any area of interest, you'd find many successful headlines written this way – with the first letter of each word set in uppercase format.

## Some Examples of Effective Titles

Here are several examples of Titles that work well in eBay Listings:

**ROLEX Men's Presidential Rose Gold MINT Private Owner**    (53 Characters)

**Massive SWIPE FILE Abraham Halbert Kennedy Nicholas NR**    (54 Characters)

**Signed Autographed Babe Ruth Baseball Ball PSA/DNA COA**    (54 Characters)

**Dan Kennedy Ken McCarthy Gary Halbert-SYSTEM VIDEOS FS**   (54 Characters)

**Wonderful 1982 PEANUTS daily - Charles Schulz Art! NR**    (53 Characters)

**John Reese Traffic Secrets-ORIGINAL! Free Shipping! NR**    (54 Characters)

**64MB Mini Spy Video, Web, DIGITAL CAMERA in 1 Free Kit**    (55 Characters)

**Gary Halbert Bob Morrison Promoter's Gold RARE Free S&H**    (55 Characters)

**Authentic New GUCCI Lady High Heel Fashion Boots Shoes**    (54 Characters)

**Truly MASSIVE Lot of Real Estate Courses: Ted Thomas** ++     (55 Characters)

**Citizen's Watch Men's Navitech JQ802052L NEW! FS NR**     (51 Characters)

Successful titles tend to use up the limited space effectively.  None of these examples had more than a few extra spaces left over.

Notice also how capitalization was used, rather than overused, in each example. A little goes a long way. In some cases it was the item that was capitalized. Another featured the power word "rare". Others emphasized "free shipping", or its abbreviated form, "FS".

Begin each word with a capital so your title reads like a headline. Then, focus on one to three words you want to highlight and capitalize those as well. Just don't overdo it.

The real secret to using your title to create tons of traffic to your listing is to understand how your target market of buyers searches for your specific item. By this I mean *keywords*. What specific words would the greatest number of prospects likely use when searching for said item? Answer this accurately and you'll know the exact words to include in your title.

It's great if you know the market well because all you have to do is uncover typical keywords you'd use in a search for a similar product. But if you're new in a particular market, it's wise to do some homework before creating and posting your ad.

The easiest way is to search recent and currently listed auctions in the same sub-category. Pay close attention to those that sold at the highest amounts as well as the sellers who continually list items in the same column. You may not yet know the market, but accomplished sellers who specialize in specific categories do and you can learn a lot of valuable information by watching how they do it. You'll probably spot a few keywords... and some glaring examples of what not to do as well, from less-successful sellers.

Getting your title noticed and clicked on is fundamental to your success on eBay. If your Title doesn't figuratively reach out and corral eyeballs inside and in massive quantities, you probably won't get as much for the item as you could or should. In other words, you're leaving money behind with a weak or ineffective title.

You want your individual line of words to stand out amongst an endless stream of similar lines. Everyone has the same space and the same rules and limitations. The difference lies in how you use it.

Getting noticed is one thing, but getting noticed by huge numbers of interested prospects willing to spend money to acquire what you've got listed is the best way to ensure maximum prices and profits on eBay.

Strive to add a magnetic pull to your message. Aside from listing the one or two major keywords prospects are likely to search for, try inserting something that's surprising, shocking, or otherwise unexpected. A shockingly low starting bid price is one technique that can work well. You need to be confident that you'll land an acceptable price in order to profitably use this technique. But when you know in advance, the appeal it creates has an almost irresistible allure.

Here's an example I used recently that drew a large audience of 384 viewers, and a sale price that earned me several hundred dollars in profit.


**$Million SWIPE FILE-- 1¢ Gary Halbert, Abraham, Kennedy** (55 Characters)

You don't have to rely on this approach by listing a "high value" item with a low starting bid. That's one way to do it. Another is to succinctly reveal the one element of your item/offer that makes it unique.

There could be dozens of sellers who've all decided to list the identical book at the same time. But the fact that your copy was personally autographed by its highly-regarded author, gives your listing added value. While the majority of book buyers are probably not interested in collectible editions, but for those who are fans of the author, your signed edition would hold more value and likely result in higher bids. So using the word "Signed" or "Autographed" in your title in this case would be a smart move.

The key is to understand how buyers search for the things they want and then to cater to those desires not just in your listing description, but in the title itself. This gives you the best possible shot of being noticed by those that matter most; serious prospective buyers with money to spend.

Another technique is to use short forms. These are wonderful space savers that help you say what you want to say in a tiny space. Commonly used short forms include:

    1¢ – One Cent

    FS – Free Shipping

    NR – No Reserve

    BIN – Buy It Now

    Rec – Recommended

    SLP – Suggested List Price

    RRP – Recommended Retail Price

The first option works great when you've got something that's worth several hundred, or even thousands of dollars. Imagine having the opportunity to snag a $5000 diamond ring for just one cent, one dollar, or even one hundred dollars.

The low list price is such a dramatic difference to the real value of the item that it's hard to ignore. "Is it stolen?" "It must be a scam at that price!" and various other thoughts would likely come to mind, and a competent seller would go to great lengths to address each and to prove the validity and legality of the offer. But at the same time, most of us are programmed to look for deals. So such an approach is sure to raise a few eyebrows.

A large number of experienced eBay buyers use, FS, NR, or BIN as part of their search criteria. If you've put these short forms to use in your title, you've made yourself visible to that pool of buyers.

Shipping costs are usually unavoidable with physical products, as opposed to digital downloads. So it's always a nice break to find an item you want from a seller who offers Free Shipping. Imagine how buyers in Hawaii, Alaska, Canada, or overseas feel about shipping charges. It can get crazy -- particularly on larger items. Free Worldwide Shipping on an item another seller charges extra for starts to look much more appealing. Obviously, your profit margin needs to be high enough to absorb these costs. But if you can do it, you're almost certain to draw a larger crowd of potential buyers.

Another element experienced buyers dislike is reserve prices. That's when the seller lists a price (not disclosed to prospective buyers) that must be reached, or the seller is not obligated to let it go. It's a cat and mouse game where interested bidders won't know if their bid is acceptable until after it is placed. With so many options for spending money online, unless you've got something that's really special or unique. Your best bet in most cases is to stick to a "No Reserve" strategy.

As is often the case, buyers don't want to wait. Once they've made the decision to purchase, it's just a matter of locating the item at an acceptable price and claiming it through the Buy It Now option.

## Key Title Concepts

It's important to think like a direct response marketer. Direct response is all about inciting favorable action. Ads are placed, mailed out, or uploaded to a website. The intention is to target a specific audience with a specific message in hopes of ultimately making the sale.

Every successful direct marketer makes testing a regular occurrence. You should too. This is particularly important if you're selling multiple items that are the same. And the easiest (and often the most revealing) element to test is the title or headline.

You might have struggled to make the best use of those 55 characters and now you're convinced that you couldn't possibly do any better. But you'll never know what combination of words brings the most traffic, bids, and dollars – until you test various editions.

Never assume that you know more than your buyers. Let them tell you in terms of results. That's the only way to know for sure.

If all you do is change the title, you'll quickly find out the title that works best for you. If you have 100 home study courses to sell, vary the headline for each of the first 5 listings. Then assess the results. Which combination brought in the most traffic... the highest number of bids... and the highest selling price?

Ultimately you want maximum profits, but one sky-high sale (a fairly common experience on eBay) doesn't necessarily mean you've got a winner. But what it gives you is a framework – a standard – from which to gauge all future results. In direct marketing, this is known as the control.

Once you've got your control, you can test against it, as you gain new insights into your product, and the buying habits and preferences of the market.

If you're a serious seller, begin to build a 'swipe file' of words, phrases and short forms. Look for good ideas used in other markets and categories and adapt them to your own purposes. You can often achieve a breakthrough with this process.

Marketing genius, Jay Abraham pioneered this technique in business. He's since taught many people to look at unrelated fields and discover what works, and then to import it into their particular industry. I'm suggesting you do the same thing by regularly exploring eBay and paying attention to the titles other sellers are using. Emulate their success.

I took one word – "recommended" – added the name of a well-known authority who had endorsed my product, and instantly saw results. It didn't just improve things once or twice. I have consistently increased the number of sales and closing prices and still use this same technique today. In this case, it was three long words well employed.

In your travels, pay particular attention to top sellers. These folks may or may not be identified as *"Power sellers"*. But whether they are or are not, they consistently get results and that's something worth reviewing.

As much you want to discover what others are doing successfully, it's also important to learn from their mistakes. Keep an eye out for any blunders that could be costing others cash. Make a note of it so you don't commit the same mistake yourself.

A common gaff is the use of keyword spamming. That's when you list your item and include what it's not, in order to get the unrelated keyword into your title and into the eBay search universe. It's against eBay policy to do this, but since eBay is only monitored by its members, it's up to each of us to report these violations. Unfortunately, many simply repeat the offence. But since the intention of most serious sellers is to live long and prosper on eBay, it's always best to strictly adhere to the official eBay code of conduct and contribute to the community as a whole.

Here's another tip on titles: avoid using words that have no direct relation to your item and are simply used to get unsuspecting browsers to click on a link. I'm talking about made-up word combinations like L@@K, or W@W, or any similar combination. No one, least of all a serious buyer, would search for these terms, nor would they expect to find utopia when stumbling upon your listing.

And the use of multiple exclamation marks or asterisks is a poor use of space. Unless you've got just a few characters left of the 55 you're trying to use up, there's really not much point in using any characters or short forms that aren't part of everyday speech or are well known and understood by your target market. If you're selling your Mercedes, "Benz" would be a suitable substitute that any prospect would understand quickly.

Consider the two-second test. That's about the maximum time that any user is going to give your title. In fact, if a prospect gives you two seconds of their time to process your title, consider yourself lucky. If your title doesn't leap off the page and grab them by the jugular, or at minimum -- raise an eyebrow, you haven't got a snowball's chance in Haiti of getting them to click, read your description, or place a bid. In short, a lack of pulling power in your title can only get in way, preventing a percentage of potential bidders from going to your page and offering their money.

You've got to reach people on a level that causes them to click-through on your title. And in many cases, you won't even have two seconds to make an impact. The key to success is to stop them cold and instigate further investigation. The best way to do that is through a combination of keywords people actually use to search for an item like yours -- combined with a dose of marketing firepower.

Perfect grammar is irrelevant, although spelling is important. Strive to get your spelling correct, but beware of any common misspellings that could be used to your advantage as well. If a word you want to use is often spelled incorrectly, try adding the most popular misspelled version at the end of your title. That way, you'll attract even more traffic.

## Proven Title Keywords

The following words have been used successfully in Titles on eBay. That's not to say they'll work every time... but may be worth testing where they're a good fit for your item. It's also worth noting that the more these (or other) words are used in a particular category or marketplace, the less effective they tend to become. Just keep that in mind as you test and consider variations and new words that spring to mind as you play around with your combinations.

| | |
|---|---|
| Antique | Discount |
| Vintage | Exclusive |
| Sealed | How To |
| Signed | Money |
| Original | Guarantee/Guaranteed |
| Rare | Fast |
| First Edition | Unusual |
| Mint | Easy |
| New | Step-By-Step |
| Free | Pain Free |
| Bonus | Freedom |
| Gift | Relief |
| Save | Instant |
| Now | Protect |
| Sale | Prevent |
| Savings | Unique |

Exciting                                    Power

Exciting — Power

Amazing — Success

Free Shipping — Most Wanted

No Reserve — Collector

Learn — Original Packaging

Do-It-Yourself

Self Improvement

## 3 Steps To Creating A Powerful Title That Attracts Attention

### <u>Step Number One</u>: *Gather Information and Collect Data*

Take your item, set it down in front of you and record as many details as they come to mind. You'll want to take this raw data and sculpt it into your description, while using key points in your title as well. So be sure to be descriptive and accurate.

List all the important and most relevant details. Consider the brand, size, color, year, model, condition, attachments, accessories like an owner's manual, and any extras like batteries, cords, or carrying cases. If it's gender-specific, be sure to note that too. Also, pay careful attention to the packaging. If you've got the original box it came in, that could add significant value to your auction.
For example, here's a small table. It's easy to gather basic information without looking too hard. So I begin a simple list...

**Type:** Small side table

**Size:** 18 inches tall

**Top:** 16-inch diameter top, with scalloped edge profile, smooth to the touch

**Style:** 4 one-piece legs made from laminated hardwood (high-grade plywood) and formed to a 90 degree bend

**Type of wood:** Top made of solid oak, legs made of hardwood ply

**Color:** dark walnut stained

**Finish:** Satin lacquered coating

**Possible uses:** beside a reading chair, night stand, plant or lamp stand, hotel furniture

**First impressions:** clean lines, sleek design, sturdy and well-built. Durable, high quality wood that looks great in the lounge or next to the wing chair

You don't have to spend a lot of time at this stage, although for more expensive items, you'll want to be sure you capture every conceivable selling point.

What happens when you discover defects or damage? Record them as well. In fact, you'll want to be sure to include an accurate description of anything that might be perceived as a flaw right up front so potential buyers know what they're really getting. The failure of some sellers to do so hurts us all in the end.

Revealing the exact damages in detail doesn't raise the value of your item. In fact, it has the opposite effect. But it does raise your credibility and this will be of much more value to you in the long run as a serious eBay seller than any losses you might have incurred by exposing the problems for all to see in your photographs and description.

While we're focused on titles in this segment, the information you're gathering will serve you well in the next phase, when it's time to write your item's description.

It's helpful once again to review your competitor's listings. Examine the information provided in their listings and decide what elements you should include too.

*Do your competitors provide the kind of information you know buyers want?*

*Do they share the important details?*

*How would you improve upon what your competitor has listed?*

When you locate direct competitors, go back to the eBay search Tool and check out their results over the past 30 days. Record any pieces of information that could help you. Look for words, popular brands in the category, details emphasized, and models that regularly fetch premium prices. Turn every visit to the massive eBay site into one of market research and discovery. Keep your eyes open and use what you discover to improve your own results.

**Step Number Two**: *Sift, Sort, and Prioritize*

Once you've taken care of step one, you should have a bunch of notes in front of you. The next step is to mine the gold and leave the waste behind. Some of the information will be valuable to you and well worth using in your listing. Other segments will be of lesser importance while some may not apply or be important enough to include.

Your task in step two is to locate the strongest words for inclusion in your Title. Look for the words and phrases that are likely of greatest interest and importance to your prospects. It's not so much what your item is that you're looking for but what words, phrases, short forms, or combination thereof will attract the attention of the largest number of prospects.

You've got to deliver in your title some of the specific things your market seeks. Therefore, any attention-getting tool needs to be tied to that interest.

Picture your typical prospect in a mad dash to find the product he wants to solve a particular problem or satisfy an emotional desire.

**What words are most likely to draw his attention?**

**What could you say to pique his curiosity so he just has to find out more?**

Your headline or title is just another billboard on the busy highway of your prospect's life. Most billboards are ignored or bypassed in a split second. Something disqualifies them as a message of interest. But your quick message (as telegraphed by your title) needs to be different. You've got to deliver the words that will stop prospects cold... and cause them to click on your link. You can't ask any more of your title than that. If it gets the click, it succeeds. If it doesn't it fails.

Go through your notes and make a new list of the most important, specific details you'd like to include in the Title. Most of your choices won't fit, so you'll need to whittle down your list. But until you have lots of words before you, it's tough to prioritize. So get them all down on paper first and then start to rank them in terms of importance to your prospects.

Consider all aspects of what your product is and what it will do for the lucky buyer who lands it. Determine what the most important specifics are such as brand, size, condition, author, model, year of manufacture, designer, material used, and so on.

If you're selling a designer handbag, the name of the designer is of supreme importance. But if you're selling a "vintage" set of kitchen utensils, the hot-pink color is what makes it most unique and it's what should be featured in the title.

Find one way to convey value, a significant benefit, or the unique qualities of your item. For example, the programmable pocket timers you want to sell could be promoted as a "marriage saver".

Assume your competition is widespread, whether that's currently fact or fiction. Your mission is to make your title just a little more interesting, intriguing, arresting, or compelling than the many others your prospect may encounter. With so little space, it's not easy to do. But the right title can make a world of difference in terms of results.

**Step Number Three**: *Compose your best combination within 55-80 characters*

Take those words you've isolated as being important and see how many you can fit into the 55-80 character window. Play around with different combinations, always striving to make maximum impact as quickly as possible. If the title is your most valuable eBay real estate… the first word of that title is the most valuable of all.

Stuff your title field with as many relevant keywords as you can, but don't overdo it. No need for commas or dashes to separate words, a single space will do. But don't omit those spaces just to squeeze in more words as you'll only be shooting yourself in the foot. If it looks like mumbo-jumbo, it will be passed over instantly.

Modify your collection of words and short forms for easy reading. Take what you have and string them together making sure your title makes sense. Many listings on eBay fail to do so. They're just a collection of words or characters that fail to woo prospects inside.

Use up as much of your allotted space as you can. Don't settle for 25 or 40 characters because that part is easy to do. Fill up the field with additional words to make the overall headline more useful, more descriptive, and more alluring. Rarely should you leave more than one or two extra spaces unused. There's always more you can say, more firepower you can inject, to potentially attract larger crowds and more active bidding.

Choose one specific word or phrase to highlight and capitalize it. When a relatively small part of your headline is placed in UPPERCASE format, it stands apart from the others. But when they're all set in uppercase, it's as if you're shouting. And that's not something you want to do in the online world.

Once you've pieced together your best effort, you're done – at least for now. Consider every effort and every listing as a test. That's what the most successful marketers do.

Chances are very good you haven't done your best headline work just yet. Instead what you have is a starting point from which to grow and improve your profits. You now have a "control" and can test new variations, once your listing is up and running.

Compare your page views and closing bid prices to that of your competitors as well as your own earlier efforts. If results are noticeably different and all other variables (no optional upgraded ad features used) are the same, carefully examine both the titles and descriptions.

## More Quick and Easy Title Tips

Knowing your product and market enough makes crafting an effective title that much easier. All you have to do is ramble off its greatest attribute or characteristic, in addition to briefly describing what it is. Think in terms of what would make your product more appealing or desirable to those who'd be interested.

If it's new, say so right up front, since most people would prefer new over used when both are affordable options. New or used, make it clear to your audience. Is it an antique or collectible? Perhaps it's a vintage item, or one that's truly rare. Again, these single words speak volumes about your item when used appropriately, so it makes sense to make room for them in your titles.

Has the car you plan to list been strictly "lady-driven", creating the perception among some that it's been used sparingly and without being pushed to the limit? If so, state it. Perhaps that Body Shop gift set sitting on the closet shelf was never actually opened and is therefore in "like-new" condition.

Knowing your market makes it easier to provide the information that will get your listing noticed. If you're selling in a genre you've been involved with for some time, you already know what the market wants.

For example, if you've worked in construction and now you're selling safety equipment to the same market, you have an inside understanding of the things that can happen on a job site and the equipment those workers would like to get their hands on. Maybe it's steel-toed boots that stay warm inside in the bitter winter months. Or perhaps it's a hard hat that won't fall off. Whatever the case may be, if you've got what they want, flaunt it. And the best way to make it known on eBay that you've got something the market wants is to reveal it in the title. That's the key to maximum exposure.

Discover what it is your market needs or wants to know before they'd even take a closer look at your item. Maybe it's the fact that the Victoria's Secret swimsuit you're offering is official VS -- and not some cheap knock-off. Or it could be that your item is brand new and 'direct from the factory' -- rather than "recycled".

Be sure to identify in one word if possible, exactly what your item is. Don't assume that because you're listed in a specific sub-section of a category that it's obvious. Sometimes the best category is an easy choice. But at other times, it's frustrating as hell trying to figure out where to run your ad. And many sellers get it wrong. So it's never a bad idea to add to your title a single word like "vase", "book", "VHS" or "desk lamp" to instantly identify exactly what the item is.

Once you have gathered a handful of words, try a few different combinations. Refine, re-organize, or rework your selection until you have a message that's accurate, appealing, and worthy of action to prospective buyers. Time spent on developing a solid title is time well invested, particularly when you have multiples of an item to sell.

*"A good title is a work of genius."*

E. Haldeman Julius
-- The First Hundred Million

# Chapter Eleven: How To Write Item Descriptions That Sell

How Much Time Should You Spend on Your Item Description?
Features and Benefits
The Only 2 Ways eBay Ads Are Processed
Stress Your Item's Unique Value
Present a Better Offer
Provide a Guarantee
Ask For Action
Add Proof

This chapter's purpose is to help any eBay seller from complete novice to seasoned pro write ads that...

**1) Generate greater interest...**

**2) Attract more bids at higher levels...** and...

**3) Net you a larger profit.**

And I'm going to help you accomplish this in as little time as possible. No small feat... so let's get started.

The first thing an eBay seller needs to be reminded of is this: when people think, they think in images. Yes, the actual pictures you include in your listing are very important and we've covered that earlier in this book. But I want you to keep that fact in the back of your mind as you write your ads.

Your descriptions will be much stronger when you write them as though no product photo existed. At this point, you want to rely only on your words. So don't hold back. Express yourself vividly.

Describe your item in detail with an injection of your own personality.

Present colorful descriptive imagery of the end result the buyer hopes to acquire by winning the item. Be sure to point out not just what it is... but what it will do for the one lucky bidder who comes out on top. Since most purchases (and high bids) are emotionally-driven, you'll be fanning the flames of desire and spreading enticing vibrations.

There are many ways to write product descriptions. There's no one way that's the best fit across the board. A condensed classified ad might work well for one item, while a multi-paged sales letter does it for another. Instead, it's best to choose a method that works well for you and with the individual item you're listing in each case.

## How Much Time Should You Spend on Your Item Description?

If you've just received a full pallet load of Olympus digital cameras, then it's probably well worth your while to create a full-fledged sales letter that covers every conceivable benefit and feature and addresses any potential questions and concerns.

With such a large quantity of the same item, it makes sense to do this because once you've created a winning listing you can simply go ahead and repeat it a number of times until you unload your entire shipment.

But for many eBay sellers, taking the time to write a sales letter doesn't make a lot of sense. If you're like most, you sell odds and ends from the basement or attic, garage sales, thrift shops, or even live auctions and estate sales. One item is often very different from the next. It might be a child's toy today and a 19th Century collectable sword tomorrow. One product means much more in potential profit than the other. Therefore, the time justifiably spent on each is not the same. Nor should it be.

Your major consideration in deciding which type of ad you'll use should be based primarily on the value of the item. If you're selling an insulated pizza delivery bag, there's a limit to its value. Let's suppose value on the high end is $50. You got it for $1 when a local pizza shop was forced to change its menu when the landlord signed over exclusive pizza rights to a giant chain. In this case, if your pizza bag was a hit, you could stand to make $49 in gross profit (less eBay and Paypal fees, etc).

From the outset, if you can make a quick $49 or so, it looks pretty good. After all, you reason, how many items sold at retail make 49 times their cost?

It may be a quick windfall, if all goes well. But even if you reach the high value, (and that's a best case scenario) how much time should you spend creating your ad? That's something you should consider with each item and then use the format that best reflects its value. You don't want to waste your time spending hours on an ad that might only fetch a few dollars. You want to maximize the value of your time and if you spend too much time selling dime store merchandise, you can't possibly make the kind of money the big dogs do.

Before you write a single word, decide how much time you'll assign to the item. It's a judgment call and only you can make it. Now it's time to bring out the one tool that will help keep you on track – your pocket timer. This simple device is an ad writer's best aid. It keeps you focused and ensures you don't spend more time than you should writing a description that stands little chance of paying you for your time.

Time has a value for everyone. I don't care if you're retired or a stay-at-home-mom with a few hours to spare each day while the kids are off to school. If you start to think of that time as a precious resource, you'll be less inclined to waste it.

OK then... now we're ready to proceed with writing the description. You've already got your item photographed and your title has been composed. It's to your advantage to also have the item you're writing about in clear view. Now, with your pocket timer by your side, open up a fresh page in your word processor -- or if you prefer, take out a note pad.

At the top of the page, paste in the title you've written.

You can use the exact title at the top of your description, or modify it into a longer, stronger headline. I recommend the second option, whenever feasible. But simply using the title at the top, or a slightly modified version of the same will do in a pinch, particularly for items of lesser value.

You can handily expand your title into a powerful headline because in the Item Description field there isn't any space limitation. So you can really spell it out in full, glorious detail here. It's the only area on eBay where you can go into as much detail as you want. So don't hold anything back, within reason, of course.

You should however be cognizant of the time spent in relation to the potential payoff. Don't invest time and mental energy that cannot pay you a healthy dividend in return.

There are numerous formulas you can use to craft a headline for any product. I'll show you some powerful ones a little later. (If you want the full scoop on writing powerful headlines, pick up a copy of my latest version of Great Headlines Instantly. I'll provide a link and more details at the end of the book.)

Let's begin with some easy first steps.


**Sample Title:**

*SCRAPBOOKING Like A Pro Scrapbook Craft Secrets CD*

Next, take the same title and paste it at the top of our Item Description

**Item Description Headline:**

*SCRAPBOOKING Like A Pro Scrapbook Craft Secrets CD*

Now consider how to expand upon this to make it more effective. If you had more space in the title field and could turn it into a lengthier version, what would you include?

Here's a quick 60-Second creation...

*New Beginner-to Expert SCRAPBOOKING Book Turns Any Novice Into A Scrapbook Pro In Just One Day! Discover The Inside Secrets of Today's Hottest Craft and Get Started Making Beautiful Memories Today! Get this book on CD today in PDF format for easy printing or reading on any screen!*

Note how we simply took the exact title and expanded it? Now that it's 3 sentences, it's more than a headline. But you get the idea. You could package this as a single headline and sub-head. Or you could use the last sentence in your body copy. The point is to see just how easy it is to provide additional product details by extrapolating the condensed title field version and creating a full headline. Without the 55-character limit, you're free to create as compelling a headline as you can muster.

Here's another example...

**Title:** How To Write A Book on ANYTHING in 14 Days Guaranteed!

**Item Description Headline:**

**Get Steve Manning's Famous Course – How To Write A Book On Anything in 14 Days or Less... GUARANTEED... And Get**

**This Expert's Step-By-Step Master Guide Used By Literally Thousands of People To Write Their Book Faster Than They Ever Thought Possible!**

**Even those who thought they couldn't put together a coherent sentence – let alone a book – are now accomplished authors. You can do it too! Here's how...**

As you now know, it's your title that has to win the click. But once it does, you want to let your prospect know that she is indeed on the right page. You've got to make a smooth transition from the title to your full-blown sales message.

Repeating the title at the top is the easiest way to accomplish this, at least to some degree. After all, those words triggered the click-through, so obviously they hit the mark. But since you're free of limitations at this point, why not take this same key information and make it into something much more alluring? That's exactly what you get with a full-out headline.

At the moment your full listing appears -- your prospect is fully engaged. She's hoping, even expecting to find something of great interest. Her curiosity has been aroused, her desire kindled. Your page opens to wide eyes brimming in eager anticipation of the payoff about to be revealed.

Now, how many times have you clicked on a title yourself, only to become quickly disinterested, disappointed, even disillusioned? Probably more than you care to remember. But you can increase your sales success by giving prospects more of what they want.

By expanding your title into a compelling headline, you continue to build your prospect's interest. And the greater the interest, the more likely it is they'll continue reading. The more of your ad they read, the more they want it. The more they want it, the more likely they are to bid. So the mission of your ad is to continually fuel interest and entice interested parties to bid or buy.

If your title gets clicked on in large numbers, there's something contained in those 55-80 characters that people want. And it's easy to measure your traffic with a simple page counter provided by eBay free of charge. The next thing is to confirm what you've got to offer and invite prospects inside where they can get the full story. So build on any interest and enthusiasm that's already present. A sold headline is an excellent way to begin.

Regardless of the time allotted, or the item you've chosen to list, the use of a headline should figure prominently into your plans.

## Features and Benefits

Now go back to the notes you made at the title writing stage. You should have a list of the most important details about your products. If you recorded such things as the brand, model number and what it's made from -- these are product details known as features.

Features are an important part of selling on eBay. With such a large and widespread market, people are interested in the particulars of one item versus another. In some cases you can get away with simply revealing your features and hoping for the best. With powerful brand names in great demand, that may be all you need. But in the vast majority of cases, you'd likely fare better with an ad that gets prospects emotionally involved. And that's where benefits play a huge role.

While features are about products, the corresponding benefits are about people. More specifically, a feature is a detail about the item itself while a benefit is what the buyer gets out of owning or using the product. It's the redeeming value the buyer gets in exchange for his or her cash.

No one buys a vacuum cleaner because they want a portable machine with an electric motor inside with a long power cord attached. What they want is a clean house. It's the end result that people really want and the most successful salespeople in all genres -- including eBay -- understand this premise fully. If you don't paint a big beautiful picture of what can easily be theirs on the other side of the transaction, you're probably leaving money on the table. It's that simple.

You don't need to examine your item under a microscope to figure out its features. If you don't already have a list of features, just start to record individual characteristics about your item. Whatever comes to mind should be captured. Better to have too much information to work from rather than not enough.

If you have more information about some items, jot that down too. That's how interesting stories are formed.

If that dart set you have for sale was only used once because of the household damage you caused with an errant shot, make note of it. What you're doing is relaying your actual experience but in the process, creating more human interest in your item than a competing ad that merely lists a few product facts.

Be sure to keep your pocket timer handy and use it as you see fit. At this stage, you're still just assembling your raw information. It will be polished up in due time, to be sure. But for now, just get it down on paper -- or on the page in your word processing program.

If you haven't already done so, simply record things like brand, color, size, weight, accessories that come with it, and so on. List these items down the left hand side of a blank page. Once completed, transform each feature into a powerful benefit. In most marketing situations, the benefits are more important than the features. But on eBay, both features and benefits are crucial to reap the maximum payoff from your listings.

You now have a list of features and a list of benefits. Many buyers want to know the specifics of your item. So having a list of the key features will satisfy them. But the benefits help strengthen those features and will help trigger bidding action and higher prices. And the benefits should help involve prospects not yet sold on the features and get them more excited and by default, more likely to place a bid.

Features are best conveyed by a simple list. You can use numbers, bullet points, even paragraph text. Or you can frame the key points in a simple box. Benefits work great as eye-catching headlines, sub-heads, or bullet points. But they can be very effective in paragraph copy too. You've seen some examples of this already.

Solid bullet points are effective sales tools to use in your descriptions. They're easy to write and they deliver a powerful marketing punch quickly and succinctly. Bullets also help break up regular paragraph copy. For the reader, this provides visual relief. A well-written bullet has the ability to grab "soft" prospects and turn them into, got-to-have-it prospects, hell-bent on coming out on top with your item when the bidding ends.

Insert sub-headings periodically, especially if your ad is longer than a half-page. Sub-heads are similar to bullet points in that they stand apart from regular text and therefore have the capacity to lure eyeballs.

Picture this: your prospect clicks on your title and your auction description page opens. Like most of us these days, your prospect is a busy guy with lots on his mind. He's interested in your item and that's why he's there when he could (or should) probably be doing any one of dozen other activities. Subconsciously cognizant of his limited time, your prospect shifts into cruise control mode to ease the mental tension. He moves through your ad but he's only half awake. But every few paragraphs, you deliver a stopper in the form of a sub-head. What a good sub-heading does is jolt the reader a bit with another compelling reason to stick to it. It's like a flagman standing on the shoulder of the highway – impossible to miss.

## The Only Two Ways eBay Ads Are Ever "Processed"

There are two ways people read ad descriptions...

### *1) They read line by line...* *or...*

### *2) They skim over the text quickly.*

But headlines, sub-heads, and bullet points are noticed by both types of readers. This makes them key components to any ad in any medium – including eBay.

Visually, they're different. Headlines should be set in type that's larger than other type in the ad. Sub-heads should be set slightly smaller than the main headline – but it's best to set them apart even more by setting these elements in a "**Bold**" typeface. Bullets are also quite different visually from the body text of your description. That in itself draws attention and combined with a compelling, headline-like message, a bullet point is a powerful element.

Sub-heads also give you another opportunity to enhance the degree of interest and desire. It's another chance to captivate, compel, intrigue, or deliver key information. In other words, it's a golden opportunity to grab the undivided attention of the skimming reader.

There's another type of sub-heading and it's offered as an upgrade by eBay. You can list this sub-head just below the title field for a small additional fee. With this option, you're given another 55 characters to supplement what you've already listed in the Title Field.  This is s prime opportunity to expand upon the title, or deliver a short, but explosive testimonial.

The downside, apart from the additional listing cost, is the fact that sub-heads are not currently included in standard eBay searches. So adding more keywords to your sub-title won't help attract any more viewers who tend to rely on the search option to find what they're looking for.

Sub-heads are generally an under-utilized tool on eBay. That in itself provides somewhat of an advantage to those who employ it. Most sellers avoid this option simply because of the added cost.

## Stress Your Item's Unique Value

This is a biggie. It's your one great opportunity to clearly discern what makes your particular item different and valuable. And you have unlimited space to do it. Describe to the eBay universe what you're offering and put some teeth into it. Sell the sizzle... so your buyer will love the steak you send.

What does your item do for buyers? In other words, what's the ultimate benefit they hope to get for themselves, should they win your auction? That's exactly what needs to take center stage in your listing. It's the perceived value that is transferred to their way when they win and it's a huge motivator in moving people to one-up another to come out on top at the closing bell.

Look for an edge. Find something unique about your item or your offer. What you really want is something that's a little different and more desirable than what the next guy is offering.

Here's an easy way to do it. Start by asking yourself the questions below and jot down the first answer that comes to mind for each.

*What is it?*

*What's great about this item?*

*What's different about its appearance, history, quality, etc?*

*What makes it faster, slower, or a consistent speed?*

*How easy is it to use, enjoy, profit from, or display?*

*What makes it perfect for your target market?*

*Is there a guarantee?*

*How can the buyer be secure in knowing that she'll get exactly what's advertised?*

*What makes this item almost perfect?*

*Why does your prospect need this?*

*Why does your prospect want this?*

*What will the buyer get from your auction that she won't get from another?*

*What makes you, your business, or your specific auction listing the right choice among the many?*

*What's different about you as a seller and why would the buyer be better off dealing with you specifically?*

Make your listing a more alluring proposition, a more advantageous choice for the buyer. There's no shortage of ways to spend money on eBay. Your task is to make spending money on your item a better option than any other available at the moment.

With a hot, in-demand item, you'll have no problem attracting traffic -- particularly with a low starting bid. Ideally, you want to create a little tension, where your prospect knows she'll have to compete to win your item. At the same time, you want to fuel their desire so they'll want it even more and you can do that by stacking one benefit or advantage on top of another.

Offering a Buy-It-Now option creates additional tension and a sense of urgency as your item could quickly be snapped up by anyone else who's willing to pay the Buy-It-Now price.

When you've got an item that's truly unique or rare, you'll find that your description practically writes itself. All you've got to do is unveil all those specific things that make this such an exceptional piece and simply go a little deeper on each point. Differentiate your item from others listed that appear to be the same.

## Present a Better Offer

Most sellers list the item as a single entity. But you can have much more success when you think of each listing as an offer and combine the original product with bonuses, a guarantee and a rock solid record of quality packaging and prompt shipping. The "offer" is an all-encompassing proposition you make to your prospect. It bundles several elements together to make your proposal much more appealing than someone else's proposal.

All those elements may or may not apply in each situation. But if you look beyond the basic item, you'll often find ways to enhance what you're presenting, making it clearly a better choice over another who simply offers the product itself.

There are two fantastic advantages to presenting "offers" rather than "items". They are...

**1) An offer creates added value...** *and...*

**2) It gives you exclusivity by making you the only source of this specific combination, bundle or proposition.**

An offer is a package deal, instead of a stand-alone item. Should a prospect weigh both, your offer should make much more sense because of everything they get out of it. It should be more appealing than the item alone, which is probably how most of your competitors would do it. You want to make it more advantageous to go with you.

Add bonus items to your listing. This isn't always easy to do. But test this approach and you'll invariably discover that eBayers will gladly pay more money for a listing that offers more in exchange.

One obvious way to add a "bonus" item is to consider any fitting accessories or packaging you have that's a perfect fit. Consider adding an owner's manual, certificate of authenticity, or even an accompanying catalog, or sales sheet that was tucked inside the original package. All these items – including the box – add to the perceived value, making your "offer" more attractive to potential buyers.

If you're really stuck, or you wish to add an extra bonus item, create a simple "hot sheet" – a list of simple tips for maximum enjoyment, use, versatility, protection, value enhancement, or profitability – from your item. You can make it as elaborate and detailed as you wish. If the content is helpful, it will help sell more people on your offer and make you more money in the process.

Just add something that will make your listing a little different. Your intention is to ramp up the motivation to own your item with extra inducements.

For example, a lawnmower with the detachable bag for clippings included carries a higher perceived value for most people than the same basic lawnmower without the bag. It's more for their money. That's the foundation you want to establish with your offer. Make it worth more, even though you may be asking much less for starters.

Consider any attachments, such as extra power cords, replacement parts such as light bulbs or heating elements, or matching touch-up paint you happen to have on hand. Any storage cases would help too. A flash drive I purchased recently came with a beautiful and elegant zippered storage bag. If I were to sell it, I'd be sure to include the bag as a bonus.

Anything you can get your hands on that would make your item worth more money to others is something you should include in your listing. I've included bookmarks and a letter from the author in book auctions I've held recently on eBay.

If you're selling information products, create a series of bonus reports, quick-start instructions, helpful booklets, or audio CD's to include in your offer. Every top information product marketer does this online and offline. If you sell these products on eBay, by all means, include extra bonuses that add value to your package.

If you're selling collectible items like movie posters or other Hollywood memorabilia, add a signed snapshot of a related star and watch you bids soar. This is a proven technique that works.

When you tap into the right resources, you can write many of these celebrities as a fan and request anything they might have with their picture on it. Some requests will go nowhere, but others will deliver a payoff. You'll have to be discreet here however. Those freebies aren't given away so you can turn around and sell them. But adding these as a free bonus can certainly mean more money in your pocket.


## Provide a Guarantee

Guarantees are powerful marketing tools in any arena and they're particularly helpful in the sometimes uncertain online waters.

Suppose you were shopping on eBay for a particular DVD. You found two auctions ending within the hour and both items were similarly priced. Both sellers had stellar Feedback Ratings. But one offered a hassle-free, 30 day guarantee. The other made no mention of a guarantee, or whether refunds were even accepted under any conditions.

Now, which listing would you be more inclined to bid on? Obvious, isn't it? You'd probably take the one with the guarantee -

- just it case. It's an extra measure of security, should you receive a faulty DVD, or experience a similar problem.

Any kind of guarantee of satisfaction will likely enhance your sales. And the longer and stronger the promise of your guarantee, the more appealing your offer becomes. Guarantees take the onus off the customer. They ensure that you deliver exactly what was promised in the listing.

Guarantee something. If you can't guarantee the item for any reason, guarantee something else. For example, you could guarantee professional packaging or shipping and/or delivery times or prompt replies to any inquires or friendly, expedient customer service.

The flexibility to return an item for a refund or credit helps alleviate any misgivings about buying or bidding on eBay. It's a safety valve that reduces anxiety while increasing active bidding.

By offering your buyers a guarantee, you remove any risk they might have had that kept them from jumping in with both feet. When you knock down enough of the reasons for saying "no" to bidding, you're in effect making it easy for prospects to say "yes". The less resistance, the more action you'll get. So find a way to guarantee something. It can only help in the long run.

Will some people take advantage of your guarantee unethically? Yes, undoubtedly that will happen. Some people will return merchandise and demand reimbursement for no reason at all. Yes, it's completely unfair. But so is life sometimes. That's just the way it is.

It's a cost of doing business and the longer you are in business and the more volume you do, the more cases you'll have where you have to deal with a guarantee. So why bother offering a guarantee when you're going to inevitably be ripped off anyway? A guarantee policy is an asset to you simply because in the grand scheme of your eBay business, you'll make more money with one than you will without.

Not all listings lend themselves to guarantee a buyer's satisfaction with the product. But you can always guarantee prompt and professional shipping and attentive and responsive customer service. The point is to utilize the power of a guarantee in a way that helps trigger more action by negating any underlying fears that could get in the way.

Whatever policy you adapt should be stated clearly as part of your listing. If it's an "All Sales Final" policy, be upfront with it. If you only accept returns if the item received is not as advertised, say so. The stronger you can make your guarantee, the less people feel at risk and the more likely they are to get involved in your auction. Just be clear in the beginning so there's less chance of problems later. Just be sure to deliver on whatever you offer in your guarantee.

## Ask For Action

It's not enough to make your presentation and leave it at that. If you don't stir prospects to action, many won't bother to follow through. It sounds silly, but even a simple command such as "Bid Now" can kick-start people into action.

After you've made your pitch and the prospect is interested, it's your job to tell him exactly what to do next. Don't assume he'll bid. Don't assume he'll mark your auction as one to watch. And don't assume he'll magically find his way back to bid later.

You've got to get him while he's hot for your item. And that moment of truth happens while he's reading or just as he finishes reading your description.

You've triggered an emotional reaction and the blood is flowing. Now, direct him to that all-important step where he can actually do something to satisfy that desire.

If your listing features a one-of-a-kind piece, now would be a good time to remind your prospect just how rare it is. If he doesn't bid now, he could miss out entirely. Same thing goes for anything in short supply. If you're down to your last 3 units of a popular kitchen gadget that's no longer manufactured, stress the near impossible task of finding another opportunity that's equally as good as the golden opportunity before him now.

Limited availability raises the perceived value of an item and it triggers a feeling of scarcity in your prospects mind. But you need to emphasize this to be sure it's not something that's easily glossed-over or forgotten about. Tell your audience what they need to do and why it's important to do so now.

A simple phrase I like to use for items regularly re-listed is this:

"With NO RESERVE, any bid can win. Don't take the chance on missing out on what is truly an outstanding bargain! Bid NOW and it could all be yours when the auction closes!"


## Add Proof

Most people are naturally skeptical of advertising claims. Therefore, any evidence you can supply that helps verify those claims can only help you.

Problem is... with most products on the market, proof is supplied in the form of customer testimonials. If you're selling odds and ends, it may be difficult to prove the validity of any claims you might make. But there are ways to add proof to your listings for many items.

If you're selling books, dust jackets and back covers are often laden with testimonials from people in the know. You can simple choose a few of these and use them verbatim, will full credit of course. Search Amazon reviews – not just for books but for consumer products of all kinds. It's possible you may just find suitable fodder for your ad copy.

If you sell products in a particular niche, start a file for product reviews you stumble upon. Search online for others. If a giant in your industry recommended a product and now you have it for sale, by all means, tell your audience who else recommended this product and what they had to say about it. Commentary from well-respected experts or authority figures in any niche market can be a powerful ally to your selling adventures of similar products on eBay.

Is your product advertised on television... or was it at one time? Be sure to mention it with the clearly understood designation, "As Seen on TV". If you're selling health supplements, find a doctor who's already recommended the product and use what they said about it to back up your own sales message.

What you're doing is adding credibility and believability to your message and the more effective you are at it, the more successful you'll be in selling on eBay.

Another strategy is to incorporate your actual Feedback comments into your Item Description. Feedback reveals more about you as a seller than it does about your product. But in my experience, people often comment on the information products I sell -- so this feedback actually provides double duty. By endorsing the product, they're in effect telling others that what they got was worth what they paid. And by leaving positive feedback, they're also implying that the seller is someone who can be trusted.

Always look for ways to add an element of proof to your listings. The more impressive the element of proof, the more likely it is to pay a handsome dividend.

# Chapter Twelve: Helpful Tips For Selling More Goods

9 Ways To More Bids and Larger Profits
Measure Results
Give Them What They Want
Sell Yourself
Create More Listings
6 Steps To Success


The purpose of this chapter is to help you make each individual listing as powerful and consistent as possible to improve your overall success on eBay.

Clarity is crucial. It's important to spell out all the details pertaining to your product, shipping and handling, refunds – if applicable, payment methods and payment instructions. If clarity is missing, the only possible result is confusion. And confused prospects don't take positive action. They'll simply leave your auction page and be gone for good.

Few people have the time or inclination to request clarification from you. Oh sure... some people may contact you to inquire. But for every person who takes this step, several others won't bother. So you've got to be sure to cross every "t" and dot every "i" or you're shooting yourself in the foot.

Review your description before you post it. Look for holes in your presentation. Any unanswered questions need to be addressed. Objections must be overcome, or at least, minimized. And any uncertainty about any key element of your product such as the year it was made, or the name of the artist who created it has to be resolved.

You want exact, to-the-point, direct descriptions as much as possible. Be sure your communication is prospect-centered rather than seller-centered. Speak in terms that matter to your audience and make your message about what it is they get out of the exchange. And make it easy to find the key information these people want to know by revealing the most important point related to your item as early as possible in your title and your description.

The easier and more direct you make the experience for serious prospects, the more likely it is that they take some form of positive action. If you can simplify and expedite the process for those who want what you have to offer, you'll stand out among the many sellers who just don't bother.

Selling on eBay is much like selling anywhere else in some respects. People tend to buy from those they know, like, and trust. An exception to this preference is when no other option is available at the time and someone really wants the item.

In this case, they're more or less forced to deal with a seller they otherwise might not. So an inconsiderate, unprofessional, or just plain ignorant seller can make the sale. But he loses out still because some people will simply walk away, rather than bid. This reduces the field of competitive bidders and holds bids to lower levels than they could have otherwise reached.

Ask any long-term seller about the secrets of their success and invariably, the discussion will include repeat business. If you repeatedly sell products in a particular niche and those who buy are happy with the products and the level of service received from you, there's a very good chance they'll come back and buy again. But you need to expand your product line in order to capitalize on repeat business.

Everything counts. Right from that first listing to the speed and quality with which you answer pertinent questions – you're being judged. People want to buy from those they feel comfortable with. So it behooves you to continuously show up in your favorite eBay categories and deliver accurate, detailed descriptions, new products and stellar service.

Deliver with consistency and people will automatically increase their trust in you. Be sure to provide the key details of each item. But don't limit yourself to a single mention of a key point in your title or buried in your description. Reinforce those important points through buyer testimonials, detail-specific photographs, or just explain it another way.

What you're actually doing is confirming the elements that are most important to your buyer. You're clearing up any hesitation due to uncertainty and you're easing any fears about the transaction that may have lingered in the buyer's mind. Repeating key details provides a level of comfort and assurance about what it is they're bidding on and increasing the odds they do just that.

Although separate fields for Shipping, Payment, and Refund details are provided by eBay, you can enhance your listings by relaying these important details within the body copy of your item description as well.

Again, repetition leads to reinforcement and increases the prospects level of comfort. It also helps people to receive the essential information, so they can instantly make the decision to move forward, without the fear of overlooking a crucial detail.

Many eBayers don't like to scroll through the entire listing. But true prospects will read your Item Description as long as it remains interesting. So placing important details such as the Payment options you'll gladly accept within your description, provides an important service to your customers. They don't have to search the whole page to get the information – its right there. They can scroll through to confirm it and strengthen their degree of trust in you.

But please make sure the details listed in one area are an exact match in the other. Remember what we said about confusion and building trust. Consistency works in your favor, but even the slightest miss can seriously hamper your best efforts.

You can maintain a level of accuracy and diligently follow all the steps to maximize your results and still end up getting questions about your listing. My advice is to simply take it in stride and be at your best level of professionalism regardless.

Some questions clearly indicate a lack of reading on the part of the questioner. But that doesn't mean they deserve less than your best level of service. Accept these challenges as yet another opportunity to demonstrate your consistency and improve the impression of you as a merchant on eBay.

First time buyers are naturally a little hesitant. If you're in a position to guarantee your product in any way, shape, or form, I urge you to do so. There's just one reason. A guarantee takes the risk away from the buyer and puts the onus on you to deliver exactly what you've promised.

I'm sure you've seen guarantees that sound too good to be true. At first glance, such a guarantee could easily be brushed off as the blatant claims of an aggressive salesperson. But when the guarantee is repeated and takes on a significant role in the description, its credibility increases. Duplication helps widen your net and increases the chances your guarantee will be both seen and appreciated. You appear more consistent and are therefore a more favorable merchant to deal with.


## 9 Ways To More Bids and Larger Profits

To achieve better results with your eBay listings, provide...

- More information...
- More visible or more accessible information...
- Extra key information that helps convert readers into action takers...

- More buying or paying options (Paypal, Money Orders, Credit Cards, Time Payments, etc.)...

- More detailed and on-target answers to any questions proposed...

- More ways to squash any fear or trepidation in buying or bidding...

- Better, faster, more accommodating services as a seller...

- Multiple ways to enhance your credibility as a seller...

- Multiple photographs of your offer...

Communicate effectively. When writing your descriptions, it's important to structure your message to make them as appealing and readable as possible. This means utilizing multiple, small paragraphs or segments instead of one gigantic one. It also means varying your sentence and paragraph length. If they're all about the same size, your reader's eyes may grow weary, causing him to click away, never to return.

Add sub-headings here and there and create a bullet point or numbered list. The easier your text is to read and the more interesting and inviting it appears – the higher the readership.

Lots of spacing makes your text more inviting and less daunting. But don't overdo it by double spacing your text, or doing something equally bizarre. After 3 or4 lines, begin a new paragraph. Toss in a short paragraph of a single line now and then. Even a single-word paragraph can grab readers and tighten your grip on them.

Subheadings break up large sections of text and provide visual relief. It's also a terrific way to deliver key information to keep prospects interested and to provide to the skimming reader, a quick overview of what you're offering. After two or three paragraphs of body copy, insert a short subheading that "advertises" the segment to follow.

Check the overall message to ensure that it's light, easy reading that can't be misconstrued. Make each section easy to grasp while gently flowing into the next.

See that your key points are prioritized for maximum effectiveness and include any important technical details. If you don't have enough information at hand about your product, look it up online.

You can enhance your message using basic HTML. An easier alternative is to use a WYSIWYG (What You See Is What You Get) editor, like NVU available for free online at - nvu.com

A few basic enhancements are all that's needed from a design perspective. Whatever you do, don't make your description look like a circus. Stick to a simple table to contain your text in a slightly narrowed format. Without it, your message will be more difficult for prospects to read. They'll receive your message in an extra-wide format if you simply type your text in the Item Description field as it appears in the form on eBay. Be sure to allow space around the frame of your table, so the text is centered with the frame itself, plus a little extra white space. This makes it more inviting to read.

Set your headlines in a larger typeface and possibly one that contrasts with the main body of your ad. For example, if your main message is set Helvetica, try setting your Headline in Times New Roman. Don't get too fancy here. Stick to basic fonts that are easy to read on the screen.

Your headline and subheadings can also be set in Bold. Subheadings should be slightly larger than the text. If you want to introduce color to your listing, do so sparingly. For example, setting your main headline and subheads in bright red, while the rest of your text is black can work very well on a white background.

Whatever design choices you settle on should enhance readability, not detract from it. Surprisingly, many sellers do just the opposite, effectively getting in the way of their own success.

It's always a good idea to standardize your accepted forms of payment, shipping and handling and your guarantee or refund policy -- and add it at the bottom of your description. That's an easy way to ensure duplication, establish consistency and enhance understanding. It also makes it easier for anyone interested in bidding.

You don't need a slick look or fancy design enhancements to succeed on eBay. In fact, slick and fancy will probably do you more harm than good. What works wonders is having items many people want and using clear, simple, descriptive language that focuses on all the things the buyer gets as a result of purchasing.

The whole secret is to make your item worth many times more in USE VALUE to prospects than they need to bid in CASH VALUE in order to secure it. Enhance desire and you increase the audience. When many people want the very item you have listed, prices can go through the roof. When that happens, life is sweet, indeed.

It costs you the same to list your item, whether or not it sells. If you don't make the sale, you still have to pay the listing fee and that's cash out of your pocket. If it sells, you also have a final value fee to pay. So even though it's remarkably affordable to advertise on eBay, it doesn't mean you'll automatically make good money.

You've got to be willing to take the steps necessary to maximize your earnings. Otherwise, you're wasting your time and your money. Your job is to deliver a message that does the selling for you and there are plenty of ways to do that here in this book.

## Measure Results

Once a listing ends, you can then analyze your ad's performance. Let's assume that you have multiple copies of the same item and you can re-list it over and over again. If you're happy with your results, you'll probably want to run the exact same ad. If on the other hand results were disappointing, making wholesale changes might be the first thought that comes to mind. My advice is to take a step back and give it some thought before rushing in and getting rid of components that could in fact be sales assets to you.

Strive for constant improvement. But look at the bigger picture before making radical changes. I've had some items go unsold some weeks and then sell like crazy the next. It's the unpredictable nature of the eBay marketplace.

Sometimes it's got absolutely nothing to do with your ad and everything to do with who shows up in shopping mode. That's not to say that you can safely assume that your first effort at advertising is your best. It rarely is.

So part of selling and growing your eBay business is to pay attention to each listing, test it, make small adjustments, and then test it again. Invariably one edition or variation will outperform all others. If you've got two versions that produce virtually identical results, run both. But have these auctions spaced a few days apart so they don't end at the same time.

The secret to testing your ads is to only make one change each time, however minor that change may be. If you opt for multiple changes, you'll never know with certainty the impact of each alteration. You won't discover the magic.

Change your title first – that's where you can make the most impact. Titles are the default search option on eBay. For most keyword searches, only titles are referenced. And in any shopping expedition on eBay, buyers are repeatedly presented with a series of titles, often accompanied by a short thumbnail image (Gallery) of the item featured.

Titles are huge. In fact, changing your title can dramatically alter your results – positively or negatively. So pay attention to your tests and always measure response in terms of page views, number of bids, selling price, and profit. Testing is the key to maximum performance.

Take any seemingly small idea and work it to the fullest. It's dirt cheap to list items on eBay... and simple testing can lead to a major breakthrough in profits, particularly where titles are concerned.

## Give Them What They Want

Success on eBay is about being able to offer what people want and making it easy for them to find your auction. Once you find the right combination, you can simply run your ad again and again, as long as you have the inventory.

Increase desire for your item by placing it within the reach of the largest pool of buyers. One surefire way to accomplish this is to start your high-value item at a ridiculously low bid without a reserve bid in place. You don't want to do this with your first-ever auction on eBay... but after you've gained sufficient experience and courage, using this strategy can pay tremendous rewards. The lower the starting bid, the wider the audience. The cheaper it is, the greater the number that qualify to buy. Sure, some people would never pay more than a few dollars. But the more people watching, the more it tends to whip others into a bidding frenzy.

Make it easy to widen your marketing net. This means opening up your sales to the global market and not limiting outgoing shipments to your own country. The fewer restrictions you set in place, the more you open up the field to potential bidders.

Financing options on more expensive items increase the reach of your listing by allowing more people to go for it. And guarantees or refund policies help overcome the fear many have to move forward. Eliminate obstacles and you'll increase action. But you need to act prudently and in a business-like manner.

The key is to know your market and to serve markets that are large enough to easily attract multiple bidders by the dozen. On the other hand, if you're selling something to a particularly narrow niche market, you most likely should not use this low starting bid strategy. With a small audience, your item will likely sell at far below its market value, leaving you with a loss instead of a tidy profit. But with popular items, this approach can be well worth it, even though it may be nerve wracking at the same time. Again, the trick is to know your audience well in advance.

Make your item more desirable by extolling its virtues. Paint vivid images of what your buyer really gets in addition to the product itself. Remember, it's those emotional benefits that often compel a prospect to buy.

Most sellers simply state a few facts about the item, add a snapshot and leave it at that. But you'll generally experience greater success on eBay if you outline the most important features, the necessary details, and then spelling out in exciting ways what it will do for the buyer.

Create a longing in your prospect's mind by detailing what ownership of your item could mean on a more emotional or personal level. Perhaps it's the unbeatable comfort he'll experience in those new Clark's loafers. Or, maybe the sheer pleasure she'll get to enjoy every time she looks at, or someone else comments on that beautiful piece of art hanging in the foyer. Or it could be the unlimited profit and sense of freedom of a family owned business that could be theirs, with the acquisition of your Start Your Own Business home study package.

Features are important elements of many successful eBay auctions. But don't rely solely on the value of your item's specific features to generate a massive bidding war and record-breaking profits for you. Be sure to point out in vivid terms, what value added benefits can be realized as a result of those specific features.

Don't limit your thinking to one benefit per feature. Get a little creative and those single benefits can easily evolve into multiple benefits, which increases your item's perceived value in the minds of the market.

Benefits are often overlooked as obvious advantages. But if a specific benefit isn't recognized as such by your audience, it's valueless. So don't shy away from pointing out what might be obvious to you. If it isn't obvious to prospects, they won't pay you for it. An invisible advantage is really no advantage at all.

## Sell Yourself

One huge secret of success is to not simply focus on merchandise, but to 'sell yourself' to the eBay community as well. Present yourself as a considerate, respectful seller who's interested in serving others. When this fundamental attitude that rings true in all you do on eBay, you'll continue to prosper, while others wallow.

A customer-friendly approach is good business anywhere and it's particularly effective in the sometimes uncertain waters of online commerce.

People love to buy but are deathly afraid of being ripped off. So the most effective way to ensure your success is to make it exceptionally easy, hassle-free and safe to do business with you.

Your credibility is your greatest asset. Anything you can do to enhance your credibility and improve your reputation should be done without hesitation. Your Feedback Rating is of utmost importance, so it's best to look at each individual transaction as a test of your service. Do your best every time out and always strive to do it even better. That's a formula for automatic success on eBay -- or anywhere else.

Provide positive Feedback for those who've given the same to you. It fosters good feelings and community spirit. Create an 'About Me' page and reveal something relevant about yourself and your business. Don't try to be something you're not but instead, be the best "you" that you can be. Stress what's unique about you or your business and then emphasize that in your day-to-day operations.

For example, let's say you're an old pro at fishing and in your eBay business, you sell fishing tackle. This is a perfect opportunity to utilize your expertise on the water and to suggest where and when specific lures or other special equipment should be used.

Tell your story on your About Me page and let potential customers get to know you. Since people tend to buy from those they know, like, and trust, you'll begin from this day forward with a huge advantage over another seller who prefers to remain incognito. Build recognition and you'll build bigger profits.

You can sell more goods by simply listing multiple auctions. Chances are you have at least two categories that would be a good match for your item, so you could potentially sell from both. You may get different results as one category often dominates another in terms of audience size and profitability, but depending on the cost of your items and your available supply, advertising in both could be well worth it.

If nothing else, you increase your exposure. That's where having a 'sign-up form' on your About Me page can really pay dividends.

Invite visitors to subscribe to your mailing list where you can let them know about any related items they may be interested in. If you specialize in a particular niche, this technique will help you build your list. It's also a means of getting double duty from each listing. So even if your auction is unsuccessful, it can still be profitable in the long run, every time you list it.

## Create More Listings

Multiple listings bring more traffic. You get more prospects and consequently, more bids and higher profits when you repeatedly list items in high to moderate demand. The effect of running multiple listings is similar to running several classified ads in a popular magazine as opposed to just one – even if the one ad was larger in size.

If you pulled out all the stops and paid a premium for a single, upgraded listing, my bet is you wouldn't do as well. You'd probably get better mileage from running multiple basic ads, than from one 'deluxe' ad with paid upgrades.

With multiple ads, it's easy to test different variations of your title. Change it up a little. Try different keywords. Reach out to the largest audience each listing category provides. Change the wording to capture the attention of different people.

Run more ads in more locations. Communicate your offerings to as many interested and qualified people as possible and you'll achieve greater results. If you've got a large supply of a particular item, try 5 different listings in as many different categories as reason dictates.

Go wherever your potential market is and don't waste time elsewhere. Run 5 different keyword-related titles and space the closing of each listing at different times throughout the week. With this approach, you're casting your net wider over the eBay landscape and chances are good that you'll hook into more anxious buyers.

Review each listing for the key components of proven advertising that works. The more of these you have in place, the stronger you make your ads. Give it your best shot every time out and always strive to do it better. That's how you can maximize your results on eBay.

## 6 Steps To Success

Follow these steps and your eBay ads will be much more successful...

**1. Create titles that reach out and capture the attention of your prospects and meets them where they are in their own thinking.** Fit into their train of thought with your interesting offer. Arouse their curiosity so they click on your title and check out your description.

**2. Establish a clear image of your offer with a succinct written description outlining the important features.** At the same time, use one or more clear photographs to pictorially convey exactly what the winning bidder receives.

**3. Provide reasons why your prospect should be most interested in your offer.** Describe in exciting detail, not what the item is... but what it will do for the buyer. It's the underlying value that adds comfort, joy, or profit to your prospect's life.

**4. Prove what you say is true.** Back up your statements with visual proof, comments from previous buyers, and/or laboratory test results. Raise the level of confidence prospects have in you. Then supply a 'safety valve' in the form of a replacement guarantee or refund and you'll expand your reach of potential bidders.

**5. Stress what's unique or rare about whatever it is that you're offering and remind prospects to take action now.** If they don't, they risk losing out on this rare opportunity forever. Hold the loss of what it is they want over their heads. It could be the loss of prestige, security, money or opportunity. Provide a reminder of the need to act at once.

5. **Tell your prospects what to do next.** If you're offering a fixed price option, try something like this -- *"Click on the Buy-It-Now option and grab it before it's sold out completely. Only 3 copies left... so you'll have to be quick!"*

eBay makes the whole process of buying and bidding super easy. But you need to kick your prospect into action immediately, or he may never come back.

# Chapter Thirteen: Key eBay Ad Copy Secrets To Help You Create Listings That Produce Results

## 7 Steps To Surefire Success As An eBay Seller

*1) Stop Target Prospects and Lure Them In.* The key is to address the right audience from the word go.

*2) Keep Them Interested.* You can only hold your prospect's attention by addressing his or her self-interest. Intensify and expand upon whatever got them to your page in the first place.

*3) Create a Desire for Ownership.* Paint a wondrous picture of what the lucky buyer gets as the end result of owning the item. It's not the item itself, but what it means.

*4) Prove That Your Item Is A Great Bargain -- Even At The Buy-It-Now Price.* Begin with a much higher value on your offer/proposition than you expect to get. Start with the regular price and reduce it step-by-step, making your starting bid or BIN price an exceptional deal in contrast to what others paid and it's true value.

*5) Give Your Prospects Reasons To Feel Comfortable and Confident in You As A Seller.* Nurture your Feedback Rating. Be attentive in your communications. And demonstrate a customer-centered business approach through your presentation and action.

*6) Make Saying "Yes" Easy As Pie.* Eliminate the roadblocks with accurate descriptions that address all possible objections/

*7) Give Prospects An Extra Push or An Extra Reason To Act Now.* Stress the uniqueness of your item, or its limited availability. Better act now before it's gone for good.

## How To Get Started Writing Your Own Moneymaking eBay Ads

*1) Motivate Yourself By Focusing on the Rewards That Can Be Yours With Effective Advertising.* At the same time, remind yourself of the pain of inaction. Recognize that eBay is your greatest opportunity to sell almost anything quickly and cost-effectively. The only way to make more money here is to list more items and make each listing as powerful as possible. This information works, but only you can make it so.

*2) Set a Realistic Time Limit and Stick To It.* You'll amaze yourself with what can be accomplished in a short period of time with focused attention and energy. You can create a solid ad in just five minutes, but sometimes it's well worth spending extra time to craft a more detailed ad. Your time investment should vary with each listing and each item. But once you set a time limitation, don't waffle. You can always reassess and adjust afterwards.

*3) Focus On Each Listing With 100% Attention.* For those 5 minutes, or whatever time you've deemed necessary or appropriate, stick to the task at hand. Brainstorm, organize, or write your ad descriptions accordingly. Most importantly, do not allow yourself to get distracted by other things.

*4) Research Your Item On eBay.* Look at the same or similar items that sold recently. Learn from these past successes and failures. Look online for related manufacturers, collectors, or special interest web sites that could provide key insights and information about your item.

*5) Start With Single Words.* Capture the words that best describe your item, or some element of it. Then shape the most appealing or descriptive words into a strong prospect-directed Title.

*6) Combine Key Facts With Emotional Benefits.* Write a description that shares the details of your item and what it can mean to the lucky buyer. Get them to feel and experience what it would be like to actually own these benefits for themselves.


## How to Make Ads More Appealing and Interesting

- Choose the right audience. Locate the specific category with the best track record of high closing bids for similar items to yours. Call out to those who are perfect prospects for your product by naming them in your Title whenever possible.

- Address only the self-interests of your biggest pool of prospects. Most people are looking for ways to solve a problem or help themselves in some way. They only spend money on what interests them at the time. Show that you understand what's important by giving your target customers what they want.

- Make your message easy to read and understand. Use short, punchy sentences and simple language. Break up your copy into easily-digested segments. And write with enthusiasm so your reader feels it. Make it easy to consume and it will be read by more potential buyers.

- Supply news. Tell readers something worthwhile, helpful, and relevant that they didn't already know. Let your prospects in on something that could give them an inside edge in their area or interest.

- Make your listing believable. The secret of creating strong appeal lies in skillful accentuation. You should never alter a fact or twist a truth. But writing benefit copy allows you to emphasize the redeeming value without limitation. That's where believability comes into play. You must make sure your benefits are believable or your prospects will simply dismiss these as advertising claims.

- Provide fast action. In this 'point and click' world of instant gratification, prospects and buyers expect quick results. Respond accordingly.

- Be specific in your descriptions. No one likes unpleasant surprises, least of all eBay buyers who get something that's quite different from what they expected. Details paint a clearer picture and help avoid unhappy situations.

- Arouse curiosity. Do the unexpected. Reveal something surprising or rare about your item, preferably in the Title. The reason? Your ad listing will stand out in any crowd and the more it does, the more eyebrows will be raised, and prospects pulled inside.

- Give your audience something of value, just for reading your description. Make them glad they stopped by. Offer helpful information or share valuable tips. Invite them to subscribe to your list to get even more. This way they win, whether they bid or not. And of course you win too, by adding to your pool of like-minded prospects.

- Leverage off famous brand names. Established brands have a reputation. Businesses have spent billions on branding. Many big name brands are held in high regard and many will buy only their favorite brand. If you're selling brand name merchandise, stress that name and you'll benefit from its' perceived acceptance – even reverence – in the marketplace. In fact, your reputation as a seller will be enhanced by association.

## How To Transition From a Short Title into a Full Description

Making a smooth transition is vital to making the most of your description. You've already caught the eye and captured the momentary focus of your target. You've created an effective "stopper" of a title as it managed to pull your prospect inside. But your ad can only succeed when the details are devoured and bids are placed.

Here are several ways to move your prospect from grabbed his attention in the first place into your sales presentation:

*1) Continue along with the message conveyed in the Title.* Whatever you said in your title worked. Those few words are important because that's what inspired the 'click'.

*2) Quote an authority.* Experts or authority figures held in high esteem by your target market can help get your ad description read. If you've got a particularly strong endorsement that your competitor's don't, consider using it or a short segment or sound bite as a transitional piece.

**3) Challenge the prospect to take action.** Tell him why only one in twenty-five readers will actually bid and question whether he's up to the task. Stress the limited availability of your item, or it's exceptionally low starting price.

**4) Emphasize all the positive qualities of the brand name.** Underscore the attributes that make it such a dominant force in the marketplace. Let billions of dollars in advertising and years of cultural acceptance work on your behalf.

**5) Expand on the keywords used in your title.** Give details freely. Hold nothing back as you expand on the short 55-character heading and convert it into a vivid description that paints an exciting visual image.

**6) Start with a great testimonial.** You may have a testimonial from a previous buyer that delivers a knockout punch. If so, use it as your transitional headline. The best testimonials convey a feeling of comfort and security in moving forward. In effect, they tell prospects, *"I was once in your shoes, uncertain and maybe a little confused. But I took the chance and I'm glad I did. Not only did I get what I bargained for, in actuality, I got so much more. Fear not, you will too."*

**7) State the benefits that only the buyer can have.** Communicate what owning the actual item means to the buyer. Emphasize the biggest benefits he gets as a result. It's this most valuable quality that's of great interest to genuine prospects and delivering this in a succinct headline ensures they'll keep reading.

**8) Tell a relevant story.** Remember the Joe Karbo ad offering the green Cadillac for sale? That was a brief story. Stories about your item add richness and value. It makes your selling argument more plausible because there's some history and personal experience behind it.

## 11 Ways To Make Your eBay Ads More Believable

You must be believed to be heard. Conviction depends on believability. It doesn't matter what you say. If it isn't believed, you've lost the sale.

Here are 11 ways to make your ads more believable:

*1) Be More Specific.* Back it up your benefit claims with facts. Focus on the exact details of your particular item. The more details you share, the more acceptable your proposition. When details are few or sketchy, skepticism sets in.

*2) Use Testimonials.* A good testimonial convincingly reveals the experience of another. You can often find product testimonials from other ads run by manufacturers or distributors. Look for sales letters, brochures, postcards, and web sites and then scour these for glowing customer testimonials that could help close more sales. With books, look to the back cover or jacket copy. Often you'll find comments from respected authorities there.

*3) Feature a Major Brand Name.* When you speak of the quality of this brand, you don't have to convince anyone. They already know it. If you're selling a top brand, you're overall pitch is more openly accepted.

*4) Reveal Even More About The Brand.* Do your research and you can uncover some interesting details. For example, you might discover the number of countries in which your product is currently sold, the total amount of one model sold worldwide, or something about the history or origin of the brand. To the already committed, it's additional fuel.

*5) Share your experience with the item.* Personalize it and it rings true. Deliver a dramatic example that illustrates the value or effectiveness of the item, or reveal the actual test results obtained from the manufacturer and it's likely to be accepted.

*6) Convey Realism.* Use actual photos of your item and not stock photos or graphic images found on the manufacturer's site or elsewhere. They may look similar, but they're not the same. Use accurate copy that describes the actual item that's up for sale, not the perfect model in a showcase.

*7) Provide proof of your item's popularity.* Quote actual results of recent auctions, or tell your story of past success – *"The last time I offered this item, my fax machine spit out orders non-stop for 3 days!"* Prove your claim with a copy of your bank statement, or an image of a recently-ended auction, showing the number of bids and the final selling price.

*8) Offer a Satisfaction Guarantee.* Give the buyer a way out and he'll be more likely to accept your selling points at face value. Give them an option, just in case they're not satisfied. That in itself communicates volumes about your own confidence in the product thereby increasing believability.

*9) Emphasize Important Points.* Use UPPERCASE letters or set them in **bold**. Repeat the key benefits. Stress the special attributes that makes your item unique, valuable, or hard-to-find.

*10) Reveal What The Experts Say About Your Product.* If the big dogs approve, surely your item must be a worthwhile purchase for anyone.

**11) Show Multiple Images of Various Views of Your Product.** Capture those specific details that help to verify the claims in your copy.

**12) Establish a Track Record As A Solid Seller.** Work hard to build and guard a favorable Feedback Rating and overall reputation on eBay and any future sales claims you make will be more readily accepted by the marketplace.

## 7 Ways To Prove Your Listing Is A Real Bargain

**1) Reveal the regular selling price.** Then display it in start contrast to your lower Buy-It-Now price and considerably lower that the Starting Bid price.

**2) Dramatize the low price in contrast to the high value the buyer gets in exchange.** For example, a book on business consulting might be promoted this way – "Million Dollar Ideas -- $9".

**3) Reveal that others have paid more and that in the near future, everyone will be forced to pay more.** "This item previously sold for $199.95 – But now it could be yours for as little as $24.95 – What a deal!"

**4) Give your audience a believable 'reason why' you're offering such a high-value item at this low price.**

**5) Reiterate that this very same item others have paid and will pay much more for is available for less – right here, right now.** Repetition reinforces the concept so it sinks in. At first glance, it might seem suspect. But seeing it again and again drives home the value of the deal before them.

**6) Build up the value of your proposition.** Increase value by identifying the important qualities such as "like new", "limited edition" that make your item worth more than another of the same. Any additional bonuses you can offer also add value.

*7) Share the experience others (who all paid full price) had with the product.* Use many quality testimonials that illustrate how satisfied these buyers are, even though they paid more than you're asking for in your auction.

## How To Get Interested Prospects To Buy-It-Now

*1) Make your Buy-It-Now price attractive.* It should be low enough (lower than retail -- or what they'd easily find elsewhere) but higher than your starting bid price.

*2) Stress the fact that the item is only available in limited quantities.*

*3) Announce the price increase that's just around the corner.* It could be a new shipment that's coming in, or the latest version of a product just released. Let them know why taking action today means they'll get a terrific bargain.

*4) Remind prospects that the clock is ticking.* Their window of opportunity is small at best (7 days with a typical auction listing) and in fact may be slammed shut at anytime should another smart buyer snap up the only available piece by beating them to the Buy-It-Now option.

*5) Offer a reward to prompt purchasers.* For example, you could offer Free Shipping with the Buy-It-Now option.

*6) Use words in your Item Description that help trigger positive action.* A few examples are... Buy NOW, Don't Miss It, Rare, Limited Opportunity, Limited Edition, Last One, etc.

*7) If you've got an exclusive product, remind prospects of the only place they can get it.*

*8) Provide clear directions.* Assume your prospect has never bought anything on eBay before. Give them simple, step-by-step guidelines on how to follow through and complete the transaction and leave as a happy buyer.

*9) Offer multiple payment options.* Paypal is great. But not everyone uses it. And until recently, you had to have your own Paypal account to use this option. If you've got your own merchant account, let everyone know that you'll gladly take their credit card payment. Also consider money orders and checks and perhaps even cash. I've accepted the latter for years and never had a problem. Conversely, I was nearly burned by a fraudulent USPS money order that looked authentic and even fooled the bank teller. So you have to be on your toes and constantly on the lookout for fake payments, just as you would in any other business.

*10) Offer a payment plan.* This is easy to do through eBay and Paypal. Allowing buyers to pay in installments places your item within the reach of more people. Most infomercials today offer "3 easy payments of just ___". The only reason they offer this is because it brings in many more customers.

## 25 Key eBay Ad Copy Pointers

*1. Know your merchandise.* Take a sincere liking to the items you're selling. If you don't value the product you're selling, it will show in your advertising. The result is that others won't value it either. No one will value your item more than you do. Let the spotlight shine on each item and sell it with pride.

*2. Find within each item some unusual or unique quality that a group of people want and emphasize that uniqueness.* Set your item apart from others that may be similar.

*3. Keep your objective in mind at all times.* You want whoever is reading your words to take action. You want them to buy now, bid now, subscribe now, or return later to take at least one of those action steps.

*4. Selling on eBay means effectively communicating with a pool of potential buyers each time out.* It's not what you know, but how you communicate. It's not what you say, or think you said – it's what your audience understands and how they react. Don't leave them in a fog. That's what matters most. Clear communication is the heart of effective advertising anywhere – including eBay.

*5. Employ the 'inverted pyramid' approach to selling.* Launch your message with your biggest guns. Start with the ultimate, most-appealing benefits designed to reach the maximum number of prospects and work your way down the list. Profit from a product's positive attributes -- without being hurt by its' weaknesses. Don't give your prospect a chance to say no before you've had the opportunity to unveil your pitch.

*6. Be alert and ready to respond at any time.* Efficiency is a key component of success on eBay. Think fast. Answer quickly. Ship your products out as soon as you've been paid. You advertise your business through courtesy, clear communication and prompt action.

*7. Gain an edge.* Be more businesslike, more helpful, more service-oriented, and more valuable to those in the market. Be more to get more. There are plenty of sellers competing for the same buyer. Give your prospects reasons enough to favor you.

*8. Get to it quick.* Whoever looks at your listing must be attracted quickly, within a few words. You need an attention-grabber your prospect can't resist.

**9. *Keep them interested.*** Visitors to your auction listing are gone the moment their interest lags. You won't sell anyone you attract to your page unless your listing interests them. To hang on to your audience, you've got to keep them interested.

**10. *Build relationships with your prospects and customers.*** Generating a sale and adding another customer is great, but having that customer come back again is even better. Treat the people you serve as friends. A successful sale gives you a one-time profit. But a "friend" may come back and buy dozens of times.

**11. *Take the pressure off.*** Ease up on the "hard sell". Let your prospects sell themselves, while you gently guide them. You only want happy customers. So keep your message clear, consistent, and sincere. Become a dependable seller. If you can, offer a money-back guarantee.

**12. *Make your buyer feel that he's the one to benefit the most.*** Make the advantages of ownership far more valuable than the cost. Let them feel as if they've won. Make the other guy feel as thought he's number one and he'll help make you a number one seller.

**13. *Lead your prospect to action.*** Provide direction and guidance. Emphasize the advantages that can only be accrued through action.

**14. *Address anticipated objections – head on.*** Objections lead to a reluctance to spend time, effort, or money.

**15. *It may be digital and seem distant at times, but eBay is a people business.*** Treat every contact, prospect and customer as a long lost relative or friend – with deep pockets.

**16. *Pile on the benefits.*** Many items sold on eBay aren't necessities by any stretch. Therefore, you need emphasize the emotional payoff in order to trigger and intensify the desire for ownership. If the 'want' is strong enough, your prospect will move mountains to get it.

*17. **Understand human behavior.*** Most people want a quick easy way to complete a task or to solve a problem. There's no shortage of things people want. And the promised results sound mighty appealing. But few want to have to work hard in order to get it. Don't force people to think. Do it for them.

*18. **Approach from the angle of your prospect's interest.*** Let him or her know in no uncertain terms that "here's something you'll be very interested in"... or, "here's what we have for you!" It's even better if you can convey this thought "here's something that will be of value to you whether you win the auction or not."

*19. **Item descriptions nobody reads do NOT help advance the sales process.*** Design your listings to communicate quickly. Make them light and breezy – an easy read. Use simple, short words and short sentences. Everyday language is understood at a glance. Speak to a readership of one. Use the word "you" often, throughout your ads. Make it a one-on-one conversation and all about what you -- the prospective buyer-- gets.

*20. **Sprinkle visual "stoppers" throughout your eBay ads.*** Sub-heads work great, as do bullet points. These are arresting devices that grab people's attention and make them want to learn more. Using lots of "white space" makes your ad much more readable.

*21. **Review past listings and take note of the results.*** Pay attention to the ones that did well and leverage those insights. Glean value from the money other sellers have already spent.

*22. **Before writing your eBay listing, review the item and its packaging.*** Look for any advertising content on the package or buried in the literature within. You may discover a golden hook – one that could mean a significantly higher profit for you.

*23. **To write your listings faster, use rapid-fire copywriting techniques.*** Deliver your biggest bang right out of the gate. Be right on the money and quick to the point. Get in there and Fight.

Throw quick punches with subheads, bullet points, or short, but powerful sentences. You've got to make your case fast.

**24. Use both factual (features) and emotional (benefits) copy.** 'Reason-why' copy tells prospects what the product is and how it works. Emotional copy is all about the payoff. Emotional copy makes a deep and lasting impact. It's the happy result that only the buyer gets to experience. A well-expressed emotional message combined with 'reason-why' thinking is a one-two punch that's difficult to resist. Use this approach in all your eBay ads – it's the greatest sales aid you'll find anywhere.

**25. Proofread your ad and title before it goes live.** Simple and innocent misspellings, typos and blatant grammatical gaffs can cost you money! A mistake with any keyword means your listing won't show up in those key-word-specific searches. If your ad rambles on incoherently, or your message just doesn't help give your item market appeal, your prospects won't finish reading, nor will they bid. Make a good impression the first time because you won't get another opportunity to knock their socks off.

# Conclusion

*"One of the most effective methods of salesmanship has always been the common or ordinary auction sale, where people establish their own price for whatever is put up for sale. Nothing compels them to buy, and they can stop bidding whenever they wish. In other words, they set their own price for whatever is being offered for sale."*

-- Maxwell Sackheim

eBay has forever changed the way the world does business. In its most rudimentary form, it might be considered an auction house. But eBay is much more than that. eBay has taken an age-old method of selling and merged this ancient concept with the new high-tech society we live in today.

Like any auction, eBay enables the buyer to choose how much they spend. It's the buyer who sets the price and can bid any amount they choose. And every buyer is free to stop bidding at any time.

Setting one's own price gives the buyer the feeling of control. Since they determine the price, it's always a great buy from their perspective. Whoever wins feels like a champion and leaves the transaction on an emotional high.

But what makes eBay such a powerful moneymaking tool for any seller is the capacity to utilize powerful, time-tested, direct-response advertising techniques with any listing. This gives you the power to make your ads as compelling as can be. It's no longer a 'wait and see' activity. Instead, advertising on eBay with these techniques is selling multiplied -- to the nth degree.

As a seller, you no longer simply place your item on display and hope for the best. The eBay machine allows you to make your strongest case and most persuasive pitch one time – and have it reach a global audience of interested buyers, over and over again.

One can only wonder at how the advertising geniuses of yesterday – folks like Maxwell Sackheim, Robert Collier, Claude Hopkins and others would have marveled at the sheer marketing clout of eBay. After all, it's eBay that places this unlimited power in the hands of anyone with a home computer, an internet connection, and something to sell. Now anyone can sell with the best of them... and reap the rewards of those top achievers.

With eBay, you can use tried and true techniques refined over the years. An instant audience of global proportions is now easily accessible. And the costs are but a mere fraction of what they were before eBay came along.

You can test your ads, tweak them, and then test again. And you can do it all for less than the price of a Starbucks' latte.

You don't need slick and flashy ads. You need accurate descriptions, powerful benefits, and lucid information your market can readily grasp. Just focus on all the things the buyer gets out of a successful transaction.

The power to profit from eBay is within your reach. It's up to you to seize it.

Get started today. Apply what you've learned here to your very next listing. Continue to absorb all you can and work at it to boost your results.

No ad is ever perfect. You can always better your best. Just give it your all... and assess the results. Then try making one change and test that. Do this consistently and your ads will continually improve.

Essentially, there are 3 ways to learn to increase your profits:

**1) Learn from what you read in books like this one...**
**2) Learn from the successes and failures of other eBay sellers...**
and...
**3) Learn from your own experiences buying, selling, and interacting on eBay and elsewhere.**

Consider each and every listing a market test. With the five minute approach, you can test the waters in any niche, without devoting inordinate amounts of your time. You know the costs... and you'll know the results soon enough.

Follow these proven ideas and you'll find it easier than ever to craft interesting, compelling eBay ads. Get started today and enjoy the pure cash profits that are easily attainable with your new ad-writing skills.

By the way, I'd love to hear how you do. Feel free to write me and share your success story using the five-minute method. If I use yours, I'll send you a valuable gift. Now start using this information to create more listings that make you more money.

With enough experience, you'll uncover what it is that makes your prospects tick. You'll figure out the underlying principles of human nature at work in your niche, enabling you to create killer eBay ads that sell more products at higher prices. Now go forth and profit like never before on eBay.

Happy selling!